Praise for

We all need true-life stories t[...] deeper, and inspire us to live [...] the extraordinary. [...] that for your soul and a whole lot more. Chuck and Hannah Keels are the real deal. Through their faith, you will be encouraged to know that God still works miracles today, and every miracle matters. From minuscule to magnificent moments individually and together, their stories will draw you in and build you up. I promise. You won't be able to put this book down until you have read through to the last page.

SUE BOLDT
Speaker, Author of *Held in His Hands* and *Refresh*

Get Up And Live is a must-read story of the unbelievable Stage 4 cancer journeys of Chuck and Hannah Keels. Their story is full of miracles and hope, as they courageously battle advanced cancer, yet—still full of joy. They aren't letting their circumstances push them around; they're having their faith guide them. There's power for all of us in this kind of clarity.

BOB GOFF
Chief Balloon Inflater, Speaker, *New York Times* best selling Author of *Love Does, Everybody Always,* and *Dream Big*

A cancer diagnosis triggers fear and uncertainty. Courageously written, joy filled and Christ centred, their testimonies spread faith, hope and love. This outstanding book will help anyone struggling with cancer or supporting others and is essential reading.

REV. EMMY WILSON
London, UK

Chuck and Hannah Keels have written a love story that will warm your heart and encourage you wherever you are in your journey of life. It's a love story about life. Life in spite of their struggle with cancer, challenges, set backs and disappointments. But it's also a love story about two people who God brought together to encourage others. When I first met Chuck and Hannah, it was them encouraging my son in law Mark and daughter

Gretchen. Mark was going through his own battle with cancer at the time. He passed April 8th, 2021. But until that day he lived life to it's fullest. It's the one message you will receive from Chuck and Hannah over and over in their book *Get Up And Live*.

They are lovers of Christ, each other and life. Anyone who meets them will be greatly encouraged by them. So curl up on a rainy day and enjoy this adventure with them. And by the way, it's not over yet. Give them a call or write them a letter and encourage them as they encourage you. Thank you Chuck and Hannah for sharing your journey with us.

PAUL E. TSIKA
Pastor, World Wide Dream Builders

God chooses to show Himself by using instruments of His grace in all of the joys and trials of life. I cannot think of better examples of a man and woman where I have seen God's attributes of long-suffering, sovereignty, and love more vividly than in Hannah and Chuck Keels. In their book *Get Up and Live*, God's power of care, mercy, healing, and comfort in the personal circumstances of both are displayed in Hannah and Chuck's enthralling and encouraging story.

As you read the book you will be overwhelmed by joy, compassion, encouragement and inspiration in seeing how God takes people going through the most difficult issues in life, such as cancer, that results in the recognition that God isn't an adversary; rather, that His hand is on all of life's situations. Hannah and Chuck advocate in their own story that the power and love of Christ will penetrate, cover and permeate any situation or circumstance. Let them show you God's love in their inspirational journey!

STU FUHLENDORF
Senior Pastor of Redemption Hills Church and
Author of *Wall Street to the Well*

Hannah has been a part of my life since I was a teenager. For me, and countless others, Hannah is not only a spiritual mentor and someone to look up to as a strong Christian, an amazing mother, and a trusted friend, but her life's work has become a road map for all that know her in how to take adversity, lay it at the feet of Jesus Christ, and use his strength to Get Up And Live.

This book IS that road map. Hannah's amazing story reveals how God restored all of these losses by giving her Chuck and by cultivating a faith drawn from a deep well of suffering. Anyone going through a life challenge should read this book. We can all use an example of how to get up and live through life's struggles.

CONOR DELANEY
Chief Executive Officer, Good Life Companies

We often search for something higher than ourselves to look for the guidance one needs to succeed at anything we do in this life with actual results. I have known Chuck and Hannah's journey up close and personal, and I would hesitate a guess that given any opportunity both will thrive. There is something special within each of these two wonderful beings that have touched my life in such a profound way that I realize the possibilities are endless. Diving into this reading about their journey and the wisdom that comes from them individually is a true winner. It is important to see it, believe it, and make it happen. With this book,I can assure you that the benefit of reading it will walk you through your journey with great support and dedication needed to succeed.

ELLIOTT SMITH
Medical Researcher Cardiac Myxomas, The Ohio State University

Chuck and Hannah take the lessons that they have learned through their hardships and use them to motivate their everyday lives. This is a book I recommend to anyone going through a hard time to inspire them to get up and live!

DAVE JENKS
Best Selling Author and Co-founder of Free Enterprise Warriors

The miraculous journey of the faith, trials
& love of two Stage 4 cancer thrivers

GET
UP
AND
LIVE

BY CHUCK & HANNAH KEELS

GET UP AND LIVE: THE MIRACULOUS JOURNEY OF THE
FAITH, TRIALS AND LOVE OF TWO STAGE 4 CANCER
THRIVERS
by Chuck and Hannah Keels
Copyright 2021 Chuck and Hannah Keels

ISBNs: 978-1-953625-15-1 Trade Paperback | 978-1-953625-17-5 Hardback
978-1-953625-16-8 Ebook

Intelligent Design Press
An imprint of Kelley Creative
Spokane, Washington, USA

Get Up and Live

The miraculous journey of the faith, trials and love
of two Stage 4 cancer thrivers

by Chuck & Hannah Keels

INTELLIGENT DESIGN PRESS

To our six sons Liam, Chucky, Lance, Daunte, Logan, and Lucas. We love you all so much.

All Glory to God for writing this story!

CONTENTS

Introduction

We can already guess what you're thinking: Stage 4 cancer thrivers are super rare. A story about two Stage 4 cancer thrivers meeting, getting married, and starting a cancer foundation to help others going through cancer is probably fiction. A study by the National Cancer Institute shows that the survival rate of a Stage 4 diagnosis is between 3-28%, depending on the type of cancer. Can lightning strike twice in the same place? The answer is yes, but it's not very likely.

The odds of Chuck meeting Hannah—with all their similarities—is incredible, and almost unbelievable. After all, both were single parents with Stage 4 cancer diagnoses, both had led healthy lifestyles until their diagnoses, both had begun coaching others through their cancer, and both were pushing to learn more about and be closer to God.

Yet this IS a true story—our story—that will take you through a journey about beating ridiculous odds and what it takes mentally and physically to push when every possibility is against you. We are sharing this story because there are some amazing lessons that we learned through pain and struggle. We pray that you never have to face cancer or a life threatening challenge in your life. We were told by God to be transparent. People need to learn the power of faith and how real strength can be acquired. Each of us have stories that blow people's minds. And then God brought us together to face adversity as a couple. Our experiences have motivated and inspired people worldwide. This story is so unbelievable that we had to write a book and share it all with you.

CHAPTER ONE

The Best Way To Start 2020

Hannah

One foot at a time, I slowly walked down the aisle. Our favorite song *Endless Hallelujah* was playing over the sound system.

I thought to myself in slight disbelief, *How did I get here?*

Don't get me wrong, I was extremely happy about marrying my best friend, but our journey to the altar was a fast one, an unexpected one, and by anyone observing from the outside in, a crazy one! If you had asked me just four months prior if I could imagine I would be getting married on New Year's Day of 2020, I'd have said that you were completely out of your mind. But here I was, pledging my life to the one and only Chuck Keels. It's quite a story and one that we want to tell together to help you understand our amazing chemistry and what a divine pairing this turned out to be.

Chuck

So many unexpected things happen in a lifetime and the older I get, the more I feel like I should understand them. I do not like when those unexpected events are bad news like a sickness, a death, a job loss. I love when those unexpected events are happy surprises like getting accepted into a school, having a baby or how about ... I'm getting married?

I have always been an early riser. The time was 4:45 am and usually, I would hop out of bed and turn on the coffee maker. But today I just lay there staring at the ceiling. There was a tiny bit of daylight starting to glow out the window with the promise of another sunny day in Phoenix, Arizona. The thoughts going through my mind at first gave me a huge smile, followed by tears rolling down my face, and then back to a smile so big I thought my face would split in two. My thoughts were about how at the ripe young age of 55 years old and having had a very confusing adult life, I was hours away from walking down the aisle to marry my best friend, the girl I had always dreamed of, and my heart was full.

Me? Chuck Keels? How did this happen?

I was head over heels in love and I could not think of anything else except being close to Hannah, experiencing life together, making memories, and growing old together. It was the relationship I never gave up on despite a previous divorce and a dating path that closely resembled a train wreck.

Hannah

My breath hitched as I gazed around the church and saw a sea of very unexpected smiling faces staring up at me. We had planned a very small wedding with our combined family of six boys, the pastor, and cousin Heather and her family. Unbeknownst to me, Chuck had invited many of our dearest friends to surprise me. The more I was getting to know Chuck Whitney Keels, the more I realized what an adventure I was getting into.

Chuck

One of the amazing things about this wedding journey with Hannah is that we had just met a few months earlier. As parents of six boys between the two of us (she has four and I have two), we would probably tell them, "Slow it down and take your time." But in reality, in that short time, we discovered the chemistry was amazing and the attraction was *very* mutual. The similarities we shared about life while dealing with cancer and our love for Jesus meant we had a strong foundation in place. We also agreed that although we knew there would be disagreements along the way, they sure wouldn't be deal-breakers.

As I learned more about Hannah, who she was inside, how people around her loved her, and how big her heart was, I realized that more of them should be part of our special day. I also thought it would be a great surprise for Hannah to walk into the church and, instead of seeing ten people, she would see all of these people who loved her. And then there were the handful of people who we had never actually met in person but who followed us on social media that also just showed up for this special day.

Hannah

Even the wedding dress I was wearing was a gift from God. I had gone to David's Bridal and tried on a few gowns, but they all felt too formal. I wanted a pretty, lacy boho-style dress but, with only a few weeks to plan our wedding, I hadn't found the right one.

The week prior to our wedding, I decided to go into *The Rack*, a store nearby our house. I have always loved looking through racks of clothing so I found my size and started pulling the tightly spaced dresses apart. I remember specifically praying to find the perfect one. As I selected a few 'off-white' dresses, I found myself pulling two dresses apart, and there it was. A beautiful off-the-shoulder, boho lace dress by Vince Camuto. My size. The perfect length. It was SO me. And it was $39. If you know anything about me, I don't spend a lot of money on myself. I had been living on a fixed income for over three years so every dollar was accounted for in my life. Don't get me wrong, I love beautiful things and eat organic food. I love quality, but I don't splurge a lot. After all, I had four teenage sons to feed, house and clothe over the past few years on my own. I had learned the hard knocks of single parenting while going through a cancer journey. I'll try not to get too ahead of myself though.

The dress was perfect. I was all set. God had met me in the little details of this wedding over and over again. From the beautifully lit candles filling up the front of the church, to a friend offering to video our ceremony as a wedding gift, and now this roomful of friends cheering us on as we embarked on our next exciting adventure of marriage.

Chuck

I have friends that spent three years planning their wedding and had to take out a second mortgage on the house to cover its expenses. Hannah and I put ours together in a few weeks and it was like a dream. As we were doing all of this planning together, I kept learning amazing things about Hannah, seeing how much we had in common, and falling deeper and deeper in love with her!

Hannah

Four months before our wedding, I hadn't even heard about Chuck Keels. I had spent the month of July 2019 escaping the summer heat of Phoenix, Arizona, by visiting my parents in North Carolina, family and friends in Pennsylvania, and spending five days in Connecticut catching up with one of my best girl friends. My two weeks in Pennsylvania were spent writing the final words of my book. I had titled it *Faith Like Skin*.

Faith Like Skin was my story of how I experienced the five major stressors of life in two and a half short years. It was through the profound losses of divorce, a major cross-country move, a breast cancer diagnosis, losing my nursing career, and my best friend to suicide, that God reshaped me. I learned to surrender my failures and losses and trust Him to be my

Provider, my Husband, and my everything. It wasn't easy, but it was worth it. I knew I needed to write down my story and the lessons I had learned from it all. Little did I know that my need to figure out how to publish this book would change my life forever.

Chuck

The wedding plans fell in place so beautifully that we knew God was at work. Redemption Arcadia, our church, looked amazing and the warm hugs from the guests set the mood. The next thing I knew I was standing front and center with our six boys with Pastor Frank next to me. The music was playing and I was watching an angel walk towards me.

As Hannah got closer, with no rehearsal, I reached out my hand to say "Welcome into my and my boys' lives."

She reached out her hand. And to me, the gesture said, "Here I am. I have been looking for you."

The ceremony was so amazing and magical. My buddy Josiah showed up with all of his camera gear to capture the moment.

Pastor Frank said, "Life is very difficult at times, but oh so beautiful," and man, was he right.

For two Stage 4 cancer thrivers, this carried an even deeper meaning. We were ready to begin our beautiful lives together.

CHAPTER TWO

Big Chuck

Hannah

After I finished writing the brunt of my book *Faith Like Skin*, I realized that I had no idea how to get it into people's hands. How in the world does someone publish a book? I shared this dilemma with my newer friend, Heather. We had met a half year prior, through the sad events of our mutual friend taking her own life. It was so unexpected and tragic. None of us knew how to navigate that incredible loss and we bonded over it and became good friends. Heather was the Children's Ministry Director at my church and was looking for some assistance to pull lessons and make sample crafts. I had homeschooled my four sons for most of their lives, so it was right up my alley. It was early August 2019 when I happened to pose that publishing question to Heather.

She thought about it and suddenly sat up with a start and said, "I don't know why I haven't mentioned it before, but my cousin just published his book last month, *and* he survived end-of-life cancer. I don't have his cell but you can look him up on Facebook. His name is Chuck Keels."

As she said this, she told me she immediately had two thoughts. It was either going to be a great introduction or a colossal flop.

Chuck Keels. I wrote down his name.

Chuck

I learned something new about Facebook. A personal page tops off at 5,000 friends. The question is, how do I know this? Let's go back a little ways so you can see and understand who I was and who I was becoming. I was born in the small town of Fostoria, Ohio. My mom and dad are Ruth and Charles and I have three brothers and two sisters. We have a close family which was cultivated by summer camping trips all over Ohio, Michigan, and Wisconsin. Birthday parties and holidays were full of friends and cousins. This upbringing not only was adventurous but also grounded us with amazing memories. We all started sports at an early age. This ingrained a competitive side so deep in me sometimes even a political discussion requires me to calm myself down. It's hard to walk away. Another thing I love about sports is listening and learning from a coach and the entire concept of a team. Everyone does their part and the team moves forward. If someone is having a tough time, others rush in and lift them up. I learned this at a young age and never forgot it.

Big Chuck

I moved to Columbus after graduation and attended The Ohio State University for two years. Because I did not have a clue what to declare as my major, and against the advice from my counselor, I dropped out of college thinking I would come back and finish. That was a big life-changing mistake. I was now in the working world and believe me when I say I did almost every job that you can imagine. I tried to go back to the local community college and did take a few classes, but I never completed my degree. So my advice is to always stay in school. Throughout my life, even though I was the hardest working job applicant, the fastest learner, and all-around best candidate for the job, my applications went in the trash because there was no college degree stapled to the resume. I soon realized I had inadvertently chosen the school of hard knocks. So that meant I needed to make myself more valuable to the marketplace.

I may not have landed the best jobs out there, but I always had one, two, and sometimes three. I enjoy hard work and I love people. A handshake and eye-to-eye contact are still as good as a signed contract. I considered myself a problem solver. I worked hard, played hard, spent money on seminars, sat in on weekend training, and climbed the ladder in my own way in this tough, demanding world. I never quit a job, but I quit a few bosses. I was what some might call *hard-headed*. This is great in some areas of life and not so great in others. I have been fired from more jobs than most people have ever had. I'm not proud of that, but in reality, it usually meant it was time to look for something better.

Years later, when I'd bump into a former colleague from ten, twenty, or even thirty years ago and they told me I had changed their life, I was blown away. I was told by friends, business associates, and even a guy in jail one time that I touched their lives and whatever I was going to be doing in life they wanted to be a part of it. Now when I look back at the confusion and the ups and downs I went through, I see how God was molding me.

Let's talk about God. I was brought up in a religious family and attended a Catholic school for eleven years. I believed that Jesus was the Son of God and was sent to forgive our sins. But I had a hard time with the part about having to go to a brick building with a short haircut, dress pants, shirt and shoes, then stand up, kneel, and somehow become a good religious guy. No, maybe I didn't like feeling boxed in. Regardless, it wasn't enough. I needed something deeper, more personal.

I attended a lot of churches in my life thanks to invitations from friends. In my younger days, the times I would thank Him for the beauty and blessings around me were usually on a hike or mountain bike trail to nowhere. Just because we wander does not mean we are lost, right? But I didn't have a personal relationship with Him. Needless to say, I definitely wasn't a religious guy—no, I was a fitness guy. Always at the gym or doing anything outdoors I could find. I stayed in such good shape that I ended up doing a little fitness modeling for 12 years.

Hannah

I've seen pictures from those photo shoots! Aw man. It's a good thing I was only in my late teens then *and* in a different state.

Chuck

Modeling gave me a goal to stay in shape and put some "walking around cash" in my pocket. I always liked having three or four hundred dollars in my wallet. I worked hard and I thought I deserved it. I was in such great shape for so long that people started calling me *Big Chuck*. Who wouldn't want to be called Big Chuck? Fitness and nutrition turned into a sales job as a supplement rep in my home state of Ohio and the doors to the world opened up. After a few trips to Arizona, Nevada, and California, and seeing the blue skies and rolling mountains, I knew I belonged in Arizona. Everyone there was a lot like me.

Phoenix, Arizona, became my new home in the mid-1990s. I did the same thing in Arizona that I did in Ohio. When I got tired of my job I would find something else: either better paying or more adventure, or both. My dating life was the same way. I got married in 1999, and the marriage itself was not the biggest life changer. The birth of my son, Chucky, and then a year and a half later, Daunte, took me to an amazing place where I'd never been before. I learned love, responsibility, and how to mold two young men. But my marriage had underlying problems which involved drinking and being dishonest on someone else's part, and six years later I became a single dad.

Jobs and relationships moved us from Arizona to California, then back to Ohio, and eventually back to Arizona after I realized deep inside that my boys needed to be around the friends they grew up with. Also, I needed to get back to the kind of outdoor work that had become my career: landscape design and installation in the beautiful Arizona Sonoran desert. In early 2015, I started to notice weird aches and pains while at my job in Ohio, but I kept working right up to the time we moved back to the Phoenix area and settled in Gilbert. I landed a job in landscape design and sales before we made the trek across the country and I hit the ground running. We even moved back to the same school district so Chucky and Daunte could be back with their buds.

I was back to working hard, going to the gym with Daunte, and playing in the dirt in my very little downtime. Hiking to watch an amazing sunrise or sunset was my favorite activity, but those hikes began to take their toll. Suddenly all the little dull pains and fatigue increased. I kept thinking I would be okay the next day when I got up, but it would be worse. Then it got to the point where one Friday night the pain outran the over-the-counter pain meds. The boys and I had gotten home from getting dinner at the food trucks in Gilbert, and I was in excruciating pain. Once the boys went to bed (they were teenagers), I went to the closest hospital to get some answers. Stumbling into the emergency room, I told them about my increased pain and they immediately started doing X-rays and scans. The first news came from an X-ray.

The ER doctor said, "You have two fractured vertebrae in your back."

I couldn't imagine that since I had not fallen. *How could this be? And who walks around with a broken back?* The doctor told me they were waiting for the CT scan results to get more information and she returned at five a.m., shut the door, and told me she had bad news.

The room went quiet and I'm pretty sure time stopped.

"Chuck, everything that is going on is from cancer," she said.

My mind went into overdrive. *Cancer? I have cancer? What kind of cancer?* Then I asked her, "How bad is it?"

The doctor said, "We don't have these answers and have to bring in a specialist tomorrow for more tests."

The additional tests were a bone marrow biopsy and a biopsy of my lymph nodes. Just in case you're wondering, a bone biopsy is done with a drill, like you get at Home Depot. They numb the area but you're wide awake watching the oncologist drill into your hip bone like he was fixing a roof.

I was sent home mumbling the word cancer and waiting for a call with the results.

Three days slowly went by. I was now on big boy pain meds, felt a constant throbbing in my back, and was fully aware that I could not make any quick movements or pain would erupt from head to toe. I finally got the call and went back to the oncologist. I was in a small room when the doctor with the holster and the Dewalt-like drill on his hip walked in and shut the door.

He said, "The results are bad."

Basically, there was so much cancer in my bones that they could not figure out the origin. They could not tell me what type of cancer I had because my body was saturated with it. I was told it was Stage 4 and I had about three more months to live.

What? I remember big tears started rolling down my face.

"There is nothing that we can do medically," they said, "Go home and be with your family."

I was only 50 years old with two boys ages 14 and 16. *How can this be?* I thought.

I went home and prepared myself to give the boys the news when they came home from school. That was nothing short of a bad dream full of hugs, tears, and a feeling of numbness. And just when I thought it couldn't get any worse, that evening I got a knock on the door and it was two hospice nurses. They sat there on my couch with tears in their eyes. They wrote prescriptions for liquid morphine, along with one for a hospital bed to be put in my living room because I could not climb the steps to my bedroom.

What was I supposed to do with only three months to live and two young boys to care for?

CHAPTER THREE

Faith Like Skin

Hannah

I went home after talking to Heather, opened up my little Chromebook, clicked on Facebook, and typed in "Chuck Keels." Whoah. I wasn't expecting videos and a big personality. I'm not sure exactly *what* I was expecting. But not a guy making juicing videos and talking about his love for Jesus! I confess I stalked him for a good hour. I went way back on his timeline and did some real sleuthing to figure out who he was. But as you know, social media isn't 3-dimensional and nobody shows everything. I admit I was curious. I really was only going to reach out to him to ask for help with publishing my book. But as I perused his profile, I had this fleeting thought that this guy could handle my story, which made me search to see if he was in a relationship. I found a LOT of selfies with women, but couldn't decipher if there was "A" woman.

"It doesn't matter," I told myself, I need help with my book, not a boyfriend.

My last relationship hadn't ended too well. Not even a year after my separation and divorce from my 21+ year marriage (one I had not ended), I found myself dating a man who I had known since I was a teenager who had also recently experienced an end to his marriage. It was a long-distance relationship that lasted 8 months. Shortly after my stage 4 cancer diagnosis, he ghosted me. He just couldn't handle my pain and his simultaneously. It felt like another rejection to me. So when I encountered the dynamic and energetic Chuck Keels on my computer screen, I knew I had to just let that fleeting thought go. I wasn't ready to sign up for yet another failed relationship. I certainly wasn't ready to open my heart to another man.

So I directed my thoughts back to figuring out how to publish my book. I had prayed to God for help and direction so I knew that this guy, Chuck, was possibly my ticket to publication. That's the kind of relationship I had developed with God. I knew in a real and personal way that He was my ultimate Provider. I asked and He directed. Over and over again, I learned to go to Him first. So it was only natural when I clicked on Messenger to compose and send a message to Chuck Keels that I prayed this prayer:

"God, if you want him to find this message if ever? I'm leaving it in Your hands."

You see, if you know anything about Facebook, a personal page can only have 5,000 friends. Chuck had reached his limit (which really made me wonder, "Who IS this man?") so I couldn't friend him. That meant my message would end up in the *other*, **other** folder and it was likely he would never see it. I really wasn't sure how tech-savvy he was. After all, he was 55, eight years my senior! I hit "send" on August 28, 2019. I looked for a response the first few days and then kind of gave up.

I had things to do, suitcases to pack.

I was getting ready to take a two-week trip on September 18, to The Netherlands to visit my cousins. I was born there in 1973, the youngest of three girls. My parents came from very large families. My dad was the oldest of seven and my mom was the second oldest of twelve kids. I have over seventy-five regular cousins, most of them younger than me. My dad was a Creative Perfumer, a fairly rare and extremely competitive profession, who excelled in creating fragrances for many products we all use and love. He created fragrances for many well-known consumer brands for personal care, fabric care, and air care products, not only for the US, but for many countries all over the world. He must have been pretty good at his profession because the American Society of Perfumers honored him in 2008 with a Lifetime Achievement Award!

I grew up smelling everything. I experienced my life from an early age through my olfactory nerves. If you put a plate of food in front of me, the first thing I do is take a deep inhale. I realize now, as an adult, how incredibly creative both my parents are and how many qualities they instilled in me. I grew up going to church, singing in the choir, attending Vacation Bible School, Sunday School, and Youth Group. I can't remember a time when I didn't believe in Jesus.

When I was five years old, my father received a job offer in New York City. My parents made the decision to leave all that was familiar to them and embark on an adventure to America. We ended up moving to Northern New Jersey where I spent the main part of my childhood into my late 20s. I attended a private Christian school, played volleyball, excelled at the trumpet, and decided I wanted to become a nurse. I attended a state university about thirty minutes away and decided to live at home and receive a car instead of living on campus.

Nursing School was hard. It was full of lengthy reading, tough exams, tons of memorization, and a lot of science. I began dating a guy from my church my Freshman year and got married around Thanksgiving of my Senior year at the age of twenty-one. Six months later, I graduated Summa Cum Laude with a Bachelor of Science in Nursing. When I finished college in May of 1995, there were hardly any nursing jobs. Since I knew that I did not want to do floor nursing, I finally found a job in the want ads in October for a position at an eye surgery center. I was legally blind without my contacts so I had a natural sympathy for anyone with vision problems. I landed the job and was trained to scrub (hand instruments to the surgeon under a microscope) and circulate (do the paperwork and make sure the surgeon and anesthesia team were doing their jobs). This job helped me secure work in every single state I lived in after that. It was a unique enough job that there was always a need for skilled nursing in this field of work. I was hired on the spot every time!

At age twenty-four, I had my very first boy and named him Liam. He was my dark, curly-haired baby. For the next 4 years, every time I had a 1-year-old, I would find myself pregnant *again*. Lance was my blonde, green-eyed baby. Logan was my brown-eyed thumb-sucker who pacified himself in every situation. And by the time baby #4 was born, we knew we had to name him an "L" name as well. Lucas was my little stinker with the biggest brightest smile. My boys were my joy. We decided to homeschool early on and the blessing of that choice was that we all bonded so well as a family. We all learned how to live in peace and understood each other. We studied everything together as a family by going on field trips, doing family unit studies on various topics, and creating fun ways to learn from our environment. It's great to see how homeschooling the boys when they were younger gave them the ability to seek out their own interests as young adults. We lived in New Jersey, Connecticut, and Pennsylvania for most of their childhood. When Lucas, the youngest, was twelve, we moved to Phoenix, Arizona. It was a big change both in weather and culture. We moved from a fairly close-knit community to a broadly spaced-out Southwest environment.

I can see now how my faith has just grown and grown through the hard stuff of life: through the difficult parts of my marriage, raising four boys (all born less than five years apart), homeschooling them, moving eight times, and surviving Bacterial Meningitis. All of that happened in just the first fifteen years of my marriage.

In 2008, I almost died from contracting Bacterial Meningitis. It started with a double ear infection and spread into my brain, which caused severe pain and seizures. My husband called 9-1-1 and an ambulance took me to the Emergency Room where the medical staff discovered my diagnosis. I have no recollection of any of it. I was in a coma in the ICU for five days before I woke up and was moved to a step-down unit for an additional five days. I was weak, had lost 15 pounds, had double vision, and lost 25% of my hearing.

But I was alive.

It took me a year and a half to get my strength back. We had to have a nanny help us for six months because the boys were still so young. My illness and recovery took an emotional toll on my marriage. Looking back now, I see that it was the beginning of the breakdown. It was also a huge boost to my faith walk. I recognized the second chance that God had given me to really *live*. It taught me where to go, later on, when even more hardships came my way.

Those hardships became the content of my book titled **Faith Like Skin**. Moving from Pennsylvania across the country to Arizona was a six-month ordeal of sorting through twenty years' worth of our possessions so we could whittle away 85% of our worldly goods. We bought a furnished house in Phoenix and filled the smallest moving truck available to take across the country. In hindsight, it was God's mercy, because only six months after moving to our new home, my husband surprised me with the news that he had been unfaithful for several years and was leaving me. Completely unexpected, we separated in February of 2016. I cried for three months straight. Divorce became inevitable, but not something I had ever considered or planned for. Just a few months later in May, I found a lump in my right breast. Assuming it was a cyst, I watched and waited for it to go away on its own. A month later, I knew I needed to figure out what it was. I found a Breast Center and made the first available appointment on July 28th.

That day changed my life forever.

It was the first day I had the "C" word mentioned to me. *Me? Cancer?*

I had been eating paleo and organic food for years and was relatively fit at my target weight, and I considered myself very healthy physically. I didn't account for the emotional upheaval that I had been through for the prior six months. The toll my broken marriage took on my health was huge. After a biopsy, I was diagnosed with Stage 3, high-grade IDC breast cancer. There are 4 stages of cancer. Stages 1-3 are considered to be treatable and 4 is thought to be "terminal" and most often referred to as metastatic, meaning that it has spread past the lymph nodes of the tumor.

Mine was a fast-growing tumor.

My surgery was scheduled for mid-October, 2016. Meanwhile, I had to move out of my house into a new apartment that God had provided out of nowhere. The boys were moving with me so we had to figure out new schooling, cars, and a brand new way of living. All of these needs "fell into place" as well. We prayed for them and God met every one of those needs.

My whole new life was just beginning. I spent five weeks recuperating after my surgery. The nursing job where I had been working on a per-diem basis called me in for a meeting and offered me a full-time job, with benefits. Again, God was providing for us. We would need those benefits the following year when the cancer spread suddenly and I would have to stop working to take care of my health. That progression of cancer caused me to be considered "Stage 4" or "metastatic," which then made me eligible for disability. The medications I was prescribed caused fatigue and several other side effects that made it difficult for me to work full time. My benefits helped cover my salary until Social Security kicked in, exactly on time. I recognized my need to let God be my ultimate Provider. When the finances didn't add up, I would receive random checks in the mail or an unexpected envelope of cash from someone at church.

There was always enough. Always.

CHAPTER FOUR

Hi ... I'm Chuck

Chuck

Along with a Stage 4 cancer diagnosis comes the fear and the thought of "What do I do with this?" Not only did the idea of "I only have three months to live" occupy my mind, but because of the pain and watching my body shut down in so many ways, I was limited to what I could do. The only real answer was to pack up the boys and get back to my family in Ohio. The biggest reason was that I had no idea of how much time I had left, so I needed to get the boys to my family. Another thought was that if I only had three months to live, I wanted to spend that time with people I loved. The move back was planned out and a plane ticket was purchased for the boys and me to fly out five days later, on a Sunday. Since the expectation was that I had only three months to live, I decided not to cart all of my stuff across the country. All of the material things like leather furniture and the flat-screen TV that I had worked so hard for now, meant *absolutely nothing*. As friends wanted to come by and say goodbye, I told them to take whatever they wanted because at the end of the week anything left over was going out to the curb as trash.

Even on the strong pain meds, I still felt ridiculous pain. That week, I saw my health decline more. I lost a few more pounds and as things we take for granted stopped happening in my body, I looked for help in things like using a coffee enema. After giving away our beds that week, we stayed at a resort that was close to the airport the night before our flight back east. The next morning, I woke up and headed down the hall towards the bathroom. I remember hearing a pop and then felt indescribable pain go through my body!

The next thing I knew, I was on the floor. I could not even get a breath.

Someone called 9-1-1. Hotel security arrived first and then the fire department. Eight guys got me onto a stretcher, down some steps, and into an ambulance. Every movement and bump was excruciating. The short ride took me to John C. Lincoln Hospital where the ER doctor ordered tests and scans, which were started right away. During the next couple of days, I was able to see the boys and my brother, Tony, who had flown in from Ohio. When he saw the bad shape I was in, he booked a second flight because he thought he would be back in a few weeks to take my body home to Ohio. No joke!

Hi ... I'm Chuck

It took two days for the medical team to gather all of the information. Two spinal surgeons, an oncologist, and the house doctor entered my room. They told me the pop and pain I had felt was a compression fracture because the cancer had damaged my bones to the point that I suffered a broken back. After reviewing everything and talking it over, they told me they had a plan. Since I had already been put into hospice, I was definitely interested in hearing a different plan.

"Your cancer is prostate cancer," the doctors informed me.

It was the first time I had heard what kind of cancer I had. The doctor continued explaining that cancer goes to where it is fed. Mine had started in the prostate and then grew into my bone marrow and lymph nodes. They told me that we needed to stop feeding the cancer by stopping my testosterone production. I would also receive a surgically implanted port so they could administer chemo and hopefully start killing the cancer as soon as possible.

After hearing "Go home and be with your family," I found this plan to be an exciting alternative!

The next day, while still in pain and on liquid morphine, I was prepped for surgery. Even though it's been six years now, I remember it like it was yesterday. They started shaving my chest where the port was going to go, administered the anesthesia and I was knocked out. Two and a half hours later I woke up in the recovery room. After I was fully awake, my docs came in and explained that the surgeries had gone perfectly.

The nurses brought me water and said, "We are taking you up to your room in a few minutes."

While I was laying in the bed thinking about cancer and my two boys, the room turned a weird frigid cold for no apparent reason. I remember scrunching up and looking to the right at the double doors because I was thinking, *Someone left them open and let the cold air rush in.* But the doors were closed. As I looked back to my left, I did a double-take. I was looking at a figure in a brown robe with a white scarf and a beard. I knew without a doubt I was looking at Jesus.

I saw His right leg take a step toward me and saw His right arm stretch out and touch my left shoulder. I heard in my head, "I've got you." I looked again and He was gone. This all happened in a few seconds.

It wasn't a doctor, a nurse, or a janitor; it was **Jesus**.

That night I had a long talk with God while I was in the hospital bed, looking at the ceiling. I was still having thoughts about my body being saturated with cancer and whether my journey was coming to an end. I did not do my normal routine of simply washing my face and turning out the lights.

To tell you the truth I was feeling sorry for myself.

Really? Cancer? I still had two boys to raise and I knew I had not come close to doing something that would make my life feel complete. I was always in bed by around nine p.m. and back up at five in the morning, ready for anything. I looked at the clock on the wall and saw nine o'clock go by, then ten, then eleven, and, yes, midnight.

Lying awake with my lights still on, I said out loud, "OK God, what gives? Is this it? Is this how it ends?"

And just as clear as anything I heard Him say, "You have been a fighter your entire life. Who are you now"?

I responded, "I am still a fighter."

And God said, "Get out of bed and wash your face. Turn off the lights. As long as you are alive, be fully alive."

Wow, did I need that. I got out of the bed, dragged my IV pole, and walked past the bathroom into the hospital hallway. At a snail's pace, with my back brace on, I walked two laps around the hospital floor. At the end of the hall was a scale. I stepped on it. One hundred and seventy-five pounds. I had lost thirty-five pounds. I barely made it back to the room. I was exhausted. I washed my face and turned out the lights.

I climbed in bed, looked up at the ceiling, and said, "Thank you, God. I needed that. I know You have been trying to get my attention so many times in my life. You have it now. If you can do this, I will completely let You orchestrate my life."

The next morning, the nurses came into my room around six a.m. and said it was time for my meds. They handed me a glass of water and these little cups. "Here are your steroids for shrinking the cancer tumors. Here are your bone strengtheners. And last but not least, your pain meds are as needed, so, how is your pain on a scale from one to ten with ten being the worst?"

I sat up in the bed, looked at the two nurses, and said, "I don't feel any pain."

The nurses said, "Order something. You were on morphine because of a broken back and your two surgeries."

I said, "I don't even like taking aspirin, I don't want to take a drug if I don't have to."

They handed me the nurse call button and said, "When the pain comes back, and it *will*,hit the button so we can get in here and get you something." Since that date, May 26th, 2015, I have never touched another pain med. The medical staff, friends, and family were all amazed.

My first chemo session was given there at the hospital. I read all of the paperwork and waited for that first treatment. Soon a nurse came into my room wearing lead protective gloves, a welder's mask over her face, and her entire body covered in scrubs. She was carrying a clear bag. In that bag was my first round of chemo. I said, "You're dressed like that and you're going to put that inside of my body?"My total stay at John C. Lincoln hospital lasted ten days and then I was moved to Hope Lodge outside of the Mayo Clinic Hospital in Scottsdale. I was there for five weeks. My family stayed close to me. I was wearing a back brace and at first, could not tie my shoes or take a shower. The chemo treatments were once a week and absolutely kicked my butt. I remember sitting up in bed and slipping on my shoes with the hope that I could walk a mile or two and watch the sun rise. I made it as far as my doorway, turned around, and made it back to the bed. I climbed back in and slept for five or six hours.

Four or five days after chemo when I felt better, I would walk into the desert which was right across the street from the front door, stretch my body a little, and have amazing clear chats with God. About the time I was actually feeling good it was time for another round of chemotherapy.

Friends and family brought the boys over a few times to visit me in the hospital, but my goal was to get back home, cook my boys dinner, take them to sports, and be a family again. I really missed my little family and I was feeling better and better each day. You should have heard my family and friends go off when I mentioned moving back home. I was not thinking that most Stage 4 cancer patients never get to move back home. And that is exactly what I did. I drove myself to chemo, rested when I had to, and on my good days went back to the gym. I was the weakest dude in the place, but I made myself go. I went to the park and walked. I got in the pool to stretch and take the weight off my body until one day I decided to try and swim to the end. Not only did I swim down and back, but by the end of the next two weeks, I was up to 20 laps a day.

Mind over matter. I prayed for strength. My favorite prayer was, "God, hold me together." After seeing the metastasized bones all over my body, every time that I tried something new I would pray that something would not break and that I would not fall apart.

I did six months of chemo because that was the doctor's plan for me. Every time I went in, they took my blood test. Next, I'd receive my three hours of intravenous drugs, and then I would go down the hall to see my doctor just to get an update. Physically I was pushing myself hard. Even harder, I was pushing myself through the mental challenge of facing a life-threatening situation. On one particular day about three months into chemo, I went in and my cancer doctor was smiling ear to ear.

"Chuck, I've studied cancer all over the world and I have never seen anything like this and I do not have an explanation. Your blood test looks like a normal healthy guy."

My journey was not of medicine, it was miraculous.

This crazy story became the contents of my book titled, *Hi ... I'm Chuck*.

CHAPTER FIVE

Brakes, Brakes, Brakes!

Chuck

After several months, I still had a couple of rounds of chemo coming up. Since most of our money was coming from a GoFundMe page, the boys and I started running out of funds. I spoke to my old employer about maybe coming back to work, and he said that if I thought I was up to it, I was welcome to return. So I did. But it was strange taking a day or two off of work to go to a chemo treatment.

Pretty soon two things started happening that made the world seem very different to me. The first was that I could not shut up about what had just happened to me. People's reactions to my story ranged from getting chills and goosebumps on their arms to tears running down their faces. I remember their hugs and walking away thinking, *I did not know that my story was so powerful*.

The second thing that happened was that I started getting emails and sometimes calls from people whose loved ones were dealing with a cancer diagnosis and someone had suggested they contact me. These individuals knew I was a Stage 4 survivor and they wanted to know what I did and how I got through the challenges. At first, the calls were a big surprise and they started out a little shaky. I would tell them my story and we would talk about the positive things I did to try and feel better, such as juicing, using frankincense oil, and taking daily walks in the park. I would hang up the phone after hearing their stories and I would be in tears. Since I was still dealing with my broken-down body, my wild emotions, and finding my new normal, I wasn't sure what I was supposed to do.

I actually said to God, "You want me to do this? This sucks! It's cancer."

God always calmly responded, "Keep going. You're getting better. You're getting stronger."

The two to three calls a month gradually increased to two or three or more a week. God started nudging me to write a book about my journey. He told me I wasn't going to get rich from the book, but it would be a tool to help others and touch their lives. With the self-publishing of my book, **Hi … I'm Chuck**, I was invited to tell my story to my classmates in Fostoria, Ohio, at our class reunion. I remember telling them that I didn't know where things were headed, but that it felt like something was going to happen. I was also invited to speak at a few churches and businesses. I remember being so excited about my clean cancer scans and being labeled NED (no evidence of disease) that I told God I wanted to tell everyone my story. I was thinking that the bigger the crowds, the more people would hear it and maybe find a little hope. God calmly responded, "I want you to talk to one person at a time." Sometimes it is tough being human. We make decisions and do things based on emotions and God knew I was not ready yet for what was about to happen.

I like to call the last five years of my life "God school." I totally surrendered my life to God and said to Him, "You are in charge. You orchestrate my life."

And I completely put it to the test.

Just ask my friends Dave and Kim out in Queen Creek, Arizona. Some days I didn't have any work on my desk, so I would get in my car and drive out to the new subdivisions because they all needed landscape designs and a yard put in. I would say, "Okay God, which way should I go? Left or right?"

The neighborhoods had beautiful new homes with dirt backyards and I would pull up, get out of the car and knock on a door. I brought up Dave and Kim because that is exactly what happened. God showed me to their front door and I rang the bell.

Dave came out and I asked, "What are your plans with your backyard?" Instead of answering my question he had one of his own. "Who are you?"

"I'm a landscape designer and installer."

He responded, "My wife, Kim and I are sitting at the kitchen table talking about the yard right now, can you come in?"

Thank you, God!

Changes, blessings, and open doors began to happen all around me. God said, "Get out the front door, nothing happens inside the house." I would walk my dog, Jax, get breakfast, and meet the most amazing people everywhere I went. I would get back to the house and think to myself, *I cannot believe who I just met and got to share my story with*! I could sense God smiling.

Now that I was starting to see my path, which was more of a cancer ministry, even dating became more difficult. It was hard enough to find someone who understood and accepted me for the big personality that I was. But after surviving Stage 4 cancer and running around talking about miracles and God, dating actually got so difficult that I told God that I was done with it. I was tired of wasting so much time that it was clearly time to focus on me and my new calling. But things weren't just happening outdoors. Something interesting was happening online in this new social media world. People from all over the world started friending me on Facebook as my story started getting out. Before long, I reached the 5,000 maximum friends that Facebook allows. Once you hit that number, you're done! People can still message you, but it goes into this weird mailbox. The reason why I say it's weird is because it's scammers and jammers from all over the world and most of them were asking for money. Regardless, I made it a point to clean out that mailbox once a month.

One late September evening, I sat down at my computer to go through the non-friend mailbox. I always skimmed them first *just in case* my rich uncle in Pakistan was sending me five million dollars. That never happened, but I did come across a message one day that I couldn't believe.

The message read: "I know your cousin Heather, I have breast cancer, I'm a single mom of 4 boys, and I am writing a book and need help publishing it."

This message had been sitting in my inbox for a month, and I was really upset because I always respond immediately whenever anyone mentions *cancer*. I finally returned that message saying, "I am so sorry I missed this. Would you be interested in having coffee and catching up?"

I finished typing the message and hit send.

Hannah

I'll never forget September 28, 2019. It was the day I received a message back from Chuck. Finally, it was *only* an entire month later that he responded with his apologetic offer to grab coffee.

"Sure!" I responded, "But you are going to have to wait two weeks until I get home from Holland."

Chuck: Holland, Ohio?

Hannah: No, Holland, as in The Netherlands.

Chuck: What? What are you doing over there?

Hannah: I was born here and I have a huge family here.

Chuck: Can we text or FaceTime until you get back?

Hannah: That would be great. But we can't FaceTime because I'm out of the country. Do you know what Marco Polo is?

Chuck: Yep. It's where you can send videos back and forth. I do not use it much but it's good for now.

Hannah

And that's when Chuck began to stalk *me* on Facebook.

Chuck

So we started communicating and I consider myself a pretty good spy. I went straight to Facebook to see who my new friend was and, like most dudes, my first impression was that she was smokin' hot! She was a single mom. Her smile lit up the screen. I knew I would learn more as we spoke and that is exactly what happened. She had busy days with family, would send amazing pictures of buildings, bridges, and beautiful architecture in Holland, and then let me know when she was free to talk.

Right away there was just something special about our conversations.

Hannah

I still remember one of the first things that Chuck messaged me.

"That breath you just took was a blessing."

That moved me. Who says that?

I began to find out exactly *who* said that and *why*. Our conversations came so naturally. It felt like, finally, somebody *got* me! He understood my cancer journey, my single parenting challenges, and my love for Jesus. It didn't threaten him. We began video chatting which brought another whole level of hilarity to our situation. I genuinely loved talking to him.

Chuck (text message)

"I'm just me. What you see is what you get, maybe I'm a little more emotional since the cancer. I feel I have a lot to give, I know I love bigger and deeper than most. I appreciate the little things in life. A child, a sunset, a flower. I'm very picky about who I date and spend my time with. I do get a little excited when I meet someone I am attracted to. It doesn't happen very often. I am okay alone because I have God. I am in a good place of calm. The question is ... what's next? What is His plan for me?"

Hannah

These kinds of comments that he texted me really made an impression on me. He was genuine, down to earth, and did not hold back his feelings. We had only been talking for eight days when he texted me the message: "Sweet dreams Mrs. Keels."

I'm pretty sure he asked me to marry him three times before we met in person only three days later. He was certain he had met his match. And, in reality, he had.

But I hadn't met him in person yet. I hadn't smelled him or touched him.

I finally headed home to Phoenix in early October. I had a layover through the Philadelphia Airport. As I was waiting for my flight, I noticed a man walking by that looked vaguely familiar. I kept my eye on him as he walked around the perimeter and headed back in my direction. I recognized him as my small group leader and husband of one of my friends at church in Arizona.

"Shawn!" I shouted above the noisy crowd. He did a double-take, not expecting to see me.

As I thought about it, it made complete sense that he was there. He was a helicopter test pilot and I knew that he had several projects in the Philadelphia area at the time. We took a selfie and sent it to his wife, chuckling about how random it was seeing each other at an airport so far from home. And then it dawned on me that I was going to meet Chuck at the Phoenix airport and Shawn would likely see me with a strange man!

"Uh, Shawn? I have to tell you something. I'm actually meeting someone I haven't met in person yet, but he's Heather's cousin. He is picking me up at the airport. We've been talking for the past two weeks."

Now Shawn is a tall broad-shouldered military guy. From what I could make of Chuck, I was pretty sure that I was a tiny bit taller than him at 5'11", but still, I had a built-in bodyguard with Shawn. I love how God had provided someone! I was so excited to meet Chuck in person now that we had been talking for a week and a half. But before that happened, I decided to download his book, **Hi ... I'm Chuck**, on my kindle to read on the plane ride home.

It was time to dig in and read his story.

Chuck

I knew Hannah's plane was coming in and I was excited to see her. At this point, it was almost funny to say "meet her in person." We had been talking and FaceTiming daily. God knew to introduce us while she was in Holland. He kept us separated because He knew me and the mistakes I made in the past just following my emotions. Our phone conversations were amazing. The best parts were learning more about Hannah's faith, her personality, and that she had the best sense of humor. I loved how witty she was. I was getting an idea of who she was and we had not even looked into each other's actual eyes yet.

This may sound crazy and completely wild, but there are some things in life you just know. The connection and chemistry were so fun that I started telling Hannah that we were going to get married and all she kept saying was, "Brakes! Brakes! Brakes!"

CHAPTER SIX

You are Second

Hannah

At last, my plane landed and I made my way towards the baggage claim area. I knew what Chuck looked like from pictures and videos, but there's just something really different about meeting a person in real life. I was walking along, pulling my carry-on, when I spotted him standing off to the side, grinning this huge smile, clutching a beautiful bouquet of flowers.

Chuck

I thought about bringing Hannah a few gifts that told her more about me and who I was. For all the guys reading this, it worked, so take note. Maybe because I'm a landscaper, flowers were first on the list along with a bundle of fresh basil from my garden. I like things with Bible verses on them so I found a journal and a coffee mug. It might be the hippy in me but I love essential oils and one of my favorite ways to wear them are on lava stone bracelets. The beads are porous and hold the oils for three or four days so I got the bracelets, dropped some lavender oil over them, and then protected them in a Ziplock bag. I did all of this knowing she might think I was goofy, but at least I would have made a new friend.I arrived at the airport a few minutes early, parked in the parking garage, walked to the baggage claim area where we said we would meet, and picked a vantage point. It was kind of like deer hunting. I wanted to get a good look at her before she saw me. She was tall, with long dark hair and her smile and eyes were amazing. She looked around trying to spot me. I thought of the scene from *Sleepless in Seattle* where Tom Hanks stays hidden, just observing Meg Ryan. I liked watching her. Hannah walked up to me, and saw my massive arms, and said..."Yes!!! I will marry you."

Hannah

Ha ha. He wished that's how the story went!

What really happened was that I spotted him and walked over and we giggled and hugged each other slightly awkwardly. After talking for twelve days straight, it was still slightly weird to meet each other in person. At least it was for me. But that lasted about five minutes. Let's just say that *Big Chuck* lived up to his name. I really liked his big arm muscles and his on-screen personality was even bigger in person. I was definitely drawn to him.

Chuck

Now we had finally met, hugged, and were close enough to at least smell each other's skin. On the way to get Hannah's bags, she said, "I ran into a friend of mine at the Philly airport. He is in my small group at church, his wife is a close friend of mine and he is going to be in baggage claim. He wants to meet you."

To me, he kind of looked like her bodyguard. Hannah introduced Shawn and he stepped in, looked me up and down to make sure I was safe and reached out his hand to shake mine. Either his chest was pretty big or he was puffing it up to look big, but the greeting ended with a smile and a "nice to meet you."

Hannah

After Chuck effortlessly hauled my suitcase off the conveyor belt, we went to his truck and settled into the seats. The first thing he did was hand me a large, heavy gift bag. A very fragrant, large, heavy gift bag. I could tell he was so excited for me to open it up and see what was inside. I've since learned that gift-giving is his love language. It's not mine, but as I opened each gift (and there were four!) I discovered they were exactly the things that I loved. There was a huge bag of fresh basil, a mug with a Bible verse that said "I will be with you always," a journal filled with Bible verses, and a very fragrant set of bracelets. Looking back I can see how each one of these gifts so accurately represented Chuck. If you asked me what my top five favorite gifts were, I would probably say each one of these. I had a cabinet full of mugs with verses on them, wrote in journals all the time, loved fresh basil, and used essential oils daily. He drove me home, pulled into my driveway, and we talked nonstop for two hours straight.

Chuck

It was as if we had known each other for years. We could have talked for hours but I knew Hannah was tired from a day of traveling. I guess I did not want to leave because that would be kind of like waking up from a dream that you didn't want to end. We could see the most amazing moon through the huge date palms in her driveway. It was such a special moment that not only did we take a selfie, but I took a picture of the moon. Now I am super glad that I did. We talked about our boys and things that were going on around us.

I kept looking into her eyes and thinking, God just put a gift in front of me that I had only dreamed about and did not see coming.

I asked Hannah if I could take her out for breakfast, to which she agreed. I tried not to act as silly-excited as I was. Now I could go home and know the dream was real. I had to drive the 45 minutes home and I didn't even care. We gave each other big hugs and agreed to meet at a favorite local restaurant in the morning. I drove off thinking about her laughter and beautiful smile.

Hannah

Our coffee date couldn't come fast enough. Once we met in person it was as if we needed to stay together in each other's presence. We recognized our 'divine pairing' early on. I had made the decision to ask God to show me every step of the way with this guy. He was unlike anyone I had ever met and if he was going to be my next husband, I was going to have to relinquish some relationship fears that I had been holding onto. That morning at coffee was the first time I got to see Chuck "in action." After all, you don't get an amazing miracle story and not share it with everyone you meet. At least not if you are Chuck and in love with Jesus. It was the first of hundreds of encounters that I would witness by just being out for coffee or a meal with him. It broadened my thinking about how to use our own stories to share Jesus. It's not that I hadn't told my own story before, but it certainly wasn't at every meal, or food store visit, or in the aisle of TJ Maxx. The most amazing part was that the longer I hung out with Chuck, I naturally became included in his story—which slowly became *our* story.

Chuck

It's this easy: God saved me from stage four cancer and then told me to tell as many people as I could. Any questions? It's that simple, especially for me. I love meeting new people and talking to them. I've done this my entire life.

"Where are you from? How did you and your wife meet? How did you end up here?"

I've always made new friends everywhere I went. I believe the second part of this equation was the number of jobs that I have had and all of the skills that came with each experience. Hannah laughs when I talk about a place that I worked and often jokes, "Is there anything you have not done?" I learned a lot from quitting a job just to move on or getting fired from a job—yes, I said fired and it's happened a few times, but always because of my big mouth and never for being late or not working hard. God told me that every single thing I did in the past prepared me for *right now*. I know you're not going to go back and read that over so I will say it again. I know that every single thing I did in the past prepared me for *right now*. Wow! Just wow! I wish I would have known *that* in those younger days every time I got fired. That would have caused me to run over and hug my boss and thank him or her because it meant another adventure was around the corner. Pretty amazing, right?

To catch you up to the present, even after six years, I still tell my story at every opportune moment. It touches lives and reminds people that Jesus is for real, He forgives our sins over and over and over and He loves us.

I have the best job in the world.

It starts with "Hey! Do you want to hear an amazing story?"

Hannah

One of our favorite memories of first "dates" occurred just 3 days after Chuck picked me up from the airport. I cooked him dinner, which is one of *my* love languages (acts of service.) Chuck pulled out his phone and started playing a song. It was one of his favorites and titled "Endless Hallelujah." It was so beautiful and a song that became incredibly meaningful to us as a couple. We sat on the couch for hours, playing each other our favorite worship songs. We had so many common interests that we started calling each other "Twinkies." (If you aren't American, Twinkies are creme-filled little cakes that come two per package.) I guess when you're middle-aged and dating, it is really important to share some major common interests. We were from different generations as I was 45 and he was 54 when we met (although he could run circles around me with all his energy).

We recognized that we obviously had some baggage from past relationships and life experiences, but the more we talked and shared our experiences, the more we realized there was enough to bond over because our relationship glue was Jesus. We had a very significant conversation in the first week that we both will never forget. I wanted to make it very clear to Chuck that he couldn't fix me or any of my brokenness.

I told him, "I already have a Savior."

As we both had come out of multiple past broken relationships, we were both natural "fixers" and had also both finally learned to go to God first with our problems.

I had no qualms about telling Chuck, "Get in line. Jesus is my First Love." I had to make that crystal clear and say it out loud.

Chuck

I was blown away at how fast things were moving with very little effort as if it was simply meant to be. This definitely was one of those situations where you have to give all the glory to God because humans cannot plan when that special person walks through the door, no matter how hard you try. God's timing is always perfect. I told Hannah that I was a lifer and if she wanted me in her life she would never have to worry about me. Hannah replied with a comment I had only dreamed about and it stopped me in my tracks.

She said, "I like spending time with you, but there is something you have to understand or this goes no further." She continued, "You have to understand that you are number two. Jesus is number one."

Hello! In seconds I went from *thinking* I was falling in love to, "I am head over heels in love with this girl!" You have to understand that the path I was on had been easily distracted by dating someone who said she was a believer, but when it came down to saying a prayer in a restaurant or God telling me to tell someone my story, she would be long gone. So when Hannah said, "You're number two." I said out loud, "Good girl!!! Where have you been my entire confused life?"

CHAPTER SEVEN

The Girl With The Fearless Tattoo

Hannah

"I think I met my husband!" I exclaimed excitedly, to Ann, my mentor at church. I wanted to tell everyone about my good news. Chuck attended church with me on the first Sunday evening together. It was another important part of my life that I needed to share with him. We decided to grab a bite to eat around the corner from the church and shared the news that we were officially dating by sending his cousin Heather, who introduced us, a selfie of the two of us together. Neither of us had shared the glorious news that we had actually even met in person so it was extra fun to shock her. Heather's reaction was priceless.

Chuck and I each had packed schedules of previously planned appointments, meetings, and his landscaping projects. We tried to fit each other into some part of every day. The fact that Chuck lived about 45 minutes away posed a time problem, so I came up with a solution. We hated saying goodbye at night, and with both of us being the kind of people who were "early to bed, early to rise," we needed to solve our problem quickly.

Chuck

"You can sleep over, but that's your bed over there," Hannah told me as she pointed to the couch. There *are* still some people out there with the morals of not sleeping together before marriage.

I said to Hannah, "I will gladly give up my bed in Gilbert for your couch in Phoenix if it allows me to spend more time with you."

Since I could generate work wherever I wanted, I was happy that the Phoenix Valley needed a good landscape designer and irrigation repairman. I ran some ads in the area and not only was I getting plenty of work, but I was meeting many more people and sharing my story.

Another thing that I loved was what happened when we sat out in the front driveway together for breakfast and dinner. We started meeting all of the neighbors who were out for a walk. It was amazing. I went from "boring busy Chuck" to having a new church family, a new neighborhood, and making new friends all while sitting next to Hannah. I was starting to see the magic produced by her big heart. When she walked into a room, the entire place would light up. The more time that we spent together, the more opportunities I had to meet Hannah's friends.

"We were praying that Hannah would meet her guy. She is so special, we wanted that for her and here you are," said Linda and Mark, a couple from our small group.

They had been praying for this for Hannah and here I was.

Hannah

Since Chuck and I are both "doers," we already had events and trips planned before meeting each other. Some we were able to do together like yoga classes, my IV treatments, and a Breast Cancer event. However, several were either out of state or out of town. Being apart for days felt strange and just plain awful. It was amazing how quickly we became inseparable. It was as if we belonged together and had always belonged together. It's just like after you give birth and then can't imagine your life without your child.

Prior to both of our trips away, I celebrated my 46th birthday and Chuck planned the entire day as a surprise. He drove me up to Sedona for a day trip. Sedona is his second favorite place to visit. (The beach is his first.) It was fun to see the area through his eyes and experience it the way he did. We hiked to Devil's Bridge in my new hikers that he gave me, took pictures, had lunch, and thoroughly enjoyed ourselves. I could imagine a future with him full of adventure. I loved change and traveling. I averaged one trip away every three months either to visit friends or family in places that I had previously lived or areas where I knew people. As I got to know Chuck, I found out he did the same thing. He was either at the beach in California or Mexico, hiking in Sedona, or visiting family in Ohio. These were more similarities that we shared, but I thought, *Was it enough*? I voiced my thoughts and primarily, my ever-present fears, to my best friend Linda. She ultimately silenced my fears of getting remarried and having to give up my freedoms of singlehood with a simple question.

She asked me, "Can you serve God better with Chuck or by yourself?"

That was it. It's exactly what I needed to hear.

It helped remind me to stop making this all about *me* and focus on what God was *calling* me to do. It became very clear.

Chuck

The list of things we had in common and said or thought at the same time is a mile long, including the fact that we both have several tattoos. One of Hannah's on her left back shoulder blade describes her perfectly. It says *"Fearless."*

We started doing just about everything together, so when I would leave for a landscaping project, I missed her a lot. I would shoot her a text or a picture of where I was and would let her know how much I missed her. I would work hard so I could get back to Hannah. Then I realized I had one more solo trip planned—a speaking event planned in Sedona. When I did these trips I would usually get in a couple of hikes. Even though I was in one of my very peaceful happy places, something was missing on that particular trip: this new special person who absorbed my heart.

Hannah already had a trip planned to Pennsylvania and North Carolina where she would be away for ten days. I decided that was enough of us having to go our separate ways – even for short periods. I was working on a little plan while she was gone so that I could surprise her when she got back. I picked her up from the airport and when we got back to my place, we went for a walk. I explained that not only had I missed her on the trip but that I had been looking for her my entire life. I told her that she was my world and I did not want to spend another second without her.

I got down on one knee and asked Hannah if she would spend the rest of our lives together and, without hesitation, she said yes!

It was mid-November.

Hannah

To me, the obvious and practical wedding date was January 1st: on New Year's Day. We certainly didn't want to wait.

What better way to start 2020 than getting married? I thought.

Once I told my parents that we were engaged, they insisted that we come for a visit so that they could meet Chuck. After all, even at 46, I was still their baby. And I wanted them to meet the man that had stolen my heart so ridiculously fast. I knew it seemed crazy to most people observing us, and even though we knew we didn't need to prove our love to anyone else, we still wanted our parents' blessing.

Chuck and I decided that if we were going to fly east to North Carolina to meet *my* parents, that we might as well fly to Ohio to meet *his* family, too. We booked our flights for early December and packed our cold-weather clothes, the ones we never got to wear at home in Phoenix during the winter. The daytime temperatures there rarely went below the 50s and the sun was always so nice and warm. We landed in Columbus, Ohio, and were warmly welcomed by his parents, and brothers and sisters. I'm sure they were surprised by how quickly our relationship had escalated, but as most people noticed, it was pretty obvious in person how much we loved each other and that we were best friends.

Chuck

We spent 3 days in Ohio introducing Hannah to family and friends and showing her a few places I enjoyed when that area used to be my home. North Carolina was going to be interesting for me because even though we had a couple of FaceTime video calls with Hannah's mom and dad, I was finally going to be meeting them in person.

Hannah's dad explained that since we weren't married yet, "We got you a hotel room around the corner and you will be sleeping there." (It reminded me of Hannah's *"You're going to sleep on the couch."*)

Despite a few first time *meet the parents* jitters, we had an amazing time. The conversation was so warm and rich and they not only welcomed me to the family, but they fell in love with my right-hand dog, Jax, who had accompanied us on the trip.

At the end of the visit, Hannah planned to head home to Arizona, and Jax and I had plans to head north to Traverse City, Michigan. I'd been coaching a guy who had pancreatic cancer and became pretty close to him, his wife, and their son, so I planned on heading there for five days. Little did I know, Jax's pass that got him on Southwest airlines had expired. When we got to the check-in counter, they refused to allow Jax on my plane. I tried to talk them into it, showed them the paperwork from my cancer doctor, and even told them my near-death cancer story, but they were not budging.

Hannah, her Papa, and I were all frustrated and I looked at her dad and said, "God's in control. He has a plan for us we don't even know about yet."

I saw him smile as if to say, "You're right."

Jax and I were able to get on the same flight as Hannah and in four hours we were home in Phoenix. I spoke to my buddy in Michigan and rescheduled that entire trip.

The next huge impending event was a marriage that surprised both us and everyone around us.

CHAPTER EIGHT

Riding in Tandem

Chuck

My livelihood was doing landscaping work. For an Ohio boy to be outside all year long designing someone's yard was a dream come true. I enjoyed the work and I enjoyed the clients. Along the way, I also started doing irrigation repair because it's a necessity in the desert and most irrigation jobs were only a few hours or a day before it was on to the next job. The best thing is that it gave me the flexibility to stop what I was doing and take a call from a cancer patient or a caregiver. Calls started coming in from all over the country because someone had been diagnosed with cancer and a friend had given them my number. They would introduce themselves to me and say that their moms, wives, or themselves were diagnosed with cancer, and then they would ask, "What did you do?" Since caregivers are going through cancer, it wasn't uncommon to hear from someone who was having a tough moment or a tough day.

I thought it was very interesting that Hannah was getting a few calls just like me. The similarities blew my mind. Because Hannah and I both had cancer journeys, we slowly became cancer coaches helping people understand their diagnoses and how to stay in the game. I would sit in the shade while on a job and chat for twenty or thirty minutes with someone who needed help. When the call was over, I'd go back to work, finish the job, get paid, and get back to Hannah.

Hannah

When I heard that Chuck was spending so much time on the phone with people listening to their experiences and trying to fill them with hope while basically "talking them off the ledge," I asked him why he had never started a nonprofit. He told me that he had started looking into it but that it seemed like an overwhelming task to him. It required a small mountain of paperwork. Chuck is definitely more of a "front office" kind of guy. Chuck's natural and God-given talents are the ability to talk to literally anyone and get them to say, "Whatever you are selling, I'm buying." Those skills were great when he was a car salesman, sold vitamins and supplements for years, and ventured into pool and landscaping design. But they weren't very useful when it came down to filling out potentially very boring paperwork. But see? That is where I come into the story. I really *don't* mind filling out forms. I love the details of finances and keeping a budget. God put me together to be the "back office" kind of girl. I'd rather *not* call someone to figure it out. As much as we were "Twinkies" about our interests, we were very different about our skill sets, in a really good and productive way. It was so cool to discover how much we complemented each other's strengths. What I enjoyed, he didn't. And what he enjoyed, I didn't. It was a divinely appointed match in this area of our lives, too.

The more we talked about the idea of starting a nonprofit, the more God impressed it as a calling on our lives. It's not every day that two Stage 4 cancer thrivers meet in middle age, have a similar cancer coaching path before meeting, and feel led by God to pursue this together. Our bond was so unique to me. We had barely known each other for a few weeks and had become the best of friends. To me, this was the stuff of movies or romantic novels, not real life.

Chuck

I have to say that I was completely in awe of how we could sit outside in front of Hannah's house for hours and talk and talk and talk. We both had different paths and experiences and we would share them, ask questions and laugh for hours. We figured out that we probably crossed paths all over the country and, without a doubt, in Phoenix over the past few years. I know I already said this, but I want to say this again. When the foundation of faith, love, commitment, and dedication was there with Hannah, there wasn't anything we could disagree about that would become a deal-breaker. And now that God was present in my life more than ever, I listened to Him. In the past, I had let the devil win a lot of battles and when I thought I was getting ahead in life or got some pleasure out of a situation, I was set back again and again. Now instead, I found myself running to the Father again and again and again. Any time something little blew up and Hannah and I had a disagreement that led to an argument, we would stop and say, "What are we doing? Let's not let the devil into our relationship." After that happened, we would cry, hug, smile and kiss and keep moving forward. Having God lead the way was new and amazing to me and I really want everyone to feel as good as I do every single day.

Another topic I want to touch on is love. Being in love. Not a codependent situation where you are relying on someone else for support emotionally or even financially. Love is amazing. Being in love is exciting and makes me always try to think of surprises to show Hannah how much I love her. One of our favorite sayings is that the honeymoon is never over. That can happen because we know and understand that our love starts with God. He loves us and we love Him and we work towards a better relationship with Him. That emotion overflows so much that people around us constantly say to us, "You guys have this glow and energy about you." We are overflowing with love from the Holy Spirit and it physically shows. Humans will let you down over and over again, but God will never let you down. Once you work Him into your life, your job, and your relationships, get ready to experience His many blessings.

Hannah

This is what made our wedding so special. Of course, we hadn't figured out all of the ins and outs as to who each of us was or how we could best love each other. That takes time and is sometimes best learned through hardships. We had no idea how many valleys we would still have to navigate. But we had been through our own very deep trials of facing our own mortality via a terminal diagnosis and the incredible loneliness that results. We both had learned how to deal with those hardships on our own, and then we started learning how to encourage each other to get through those tough times. God had given us the imagery of a triangle, where He was at the top and we were each at the bottom corners. To work together, and do it well, we had to both be looking up and moving towards Him. It was a beautiful picture and one that we brought into our vows. We proclaimed our unending love to each other and took communion not only in front of a church full of people but before our parents who were watching a live feed on their devices from their own homes in Ohio and North Carolina. We recognized that this was a sacred promise to God, to be faithful and to love each other, no matter what. We had both come out of broken marriages and had no interest in repeating past mistakes.

God had brought each of us to a new place, one of wanting to honor Him first and foremost in our relationship. It changed everything. It made the candlelit kiss all the more special when Pastor Frank announced us as Mr. and Mrs. Keels.

Chuck

Remember back when I mentioned that my buddy Josiah, who is a professional photographer, showed up at the wedding with all of his camera equipment and drones? He produced the most amazing wedding music video and gave it to us as a gift. One of the things I love about Josiah's video is we are all busy with specific tasks. My job was setting things up, getting people in place, and greeting the guests. When I watched the wedding video a month later and saw all of the things going on around me, I was blown away. The smiles, our six boys standing up for us, our parents on video calls, and Jax running around the church with our rings tied to his neck. It was the video that gave me the big picture. It became a huge reminder of how God's plan could not have been more perfect.

Anything could have gone wrong with a wedding that was planned in a little less than six weeks. We have all watched entertaining wedding fail videos. Ours was *not* one of them. It was perfect. I had the feeling of being exactly where I was supposed to be at that specific moment in time. If you have never had that feeling, search for it. Pray for it.

Hannah

Chuck had arranged for us to borrow our friend's vintage tandem bike. It was white with wood accents and he called it our limo.

It became the vehicle for one of the best rides of my life.

Chuck

Prior to the ceremony, I borrowed a tandem bike from my friends, Allison and Shawn. When they asked what I needed it for, I told them I was going to church to pick up my wife. We laughed at the time, but that's exactly what I did. After the ceremony was over, everyone gathered outside for our departure. I pulled up on this tandem bike that had tin cans hanging from it and a sign that said: "just married." With cameras rolling, Hannah hopped on the back as Jax chased us around the parking lot. I did exactly what I had planned and rode the few blocks back to our house with my girl. My excitement and adrenaline were so high she didn't even have to help pedal.

Riding home together. Starting a life together.

Partnering with someone: the partner that I had been dreaming about for so, so long.

Hannah

We were living in a rental three blocks from the church, a house that God had provided for me and my four boys one and a half years prior. I loved living near my church. It had provided me the ability to serve in several ways without the excuse of being too far away. The medication that I was taking for metastatic breast cancer often gave me fatigue, something I was learning to push through because I was realizing that I probably wouldn't do anything if I caved into it. So the fact that I lived so close gave me opportunities to help run the Women's Ministry Events, serve as a greeter, and help with the Children's Ministry—the very way that God introduced Chuck to me. It still doesn't escape me that it was through *service to others* that I met him. It was through giving up small parts of my life, that I found my new husband. I had decided, after hearing a message about singleness, to be the very best single I could be. My sons were growing up and not at home most of the time because of jobs and school. It left me alone and lonely. Because I was on disability due to my diagnosis, I had a lot more free time. God was leading me through a season of learning my new calling in my present circumstances. It was one of serving others in a new way, using my God-given talents *and* my acquired skills. After losing my career as a nurse, I had a real sense of loss of purpose and calling. I had to actively pursue what my next "job" in life was for me, and I found it through asking God. It wasn't a permanent calling, but I see now how He was preparing me to serve *with* Chuck.

So getting on that tandem with him on our wedding day and pushing each pedal together, in the same forward motion, meant a lot more than just a ride back home. It was a beautiful symbol of our newly acquired "oneness" before God, our friends, and our families. The term "family" had expanded significantly for each of us. We had new parents, brothers and sisters, nephews and nieces, and most importantly, new sons. Six boys. They were literally in age order between the two of us. One year apart. Only God plans those details. Although the youngest was almost 17, and his brothers were living on their own, we still felt the responsibility of connecting our boys together. We planned to have our "reception" at a nearby restaurant with all of our boys. It was full of laughter and a fun way to celebrate a new beginning for our family. It was the start of a new year: 2020. A year that would change all of our lives.

CHAPTER NINE

The Honeymoon Is Never Over

Chuck

I was starting to learn that my new partner in life was a great planner and packer. This action started three to five days before we embarked on a new adventure. This was one of the many appreciated talents that came with the deal. The wedding was planned so fast that we did not even have a formal reception. But that didn't mean there was no celebration. We sat down together with a bottle of champagne and lit a bunch of the candles we brought back from the ceremony. Then we opened the unexpected gifts our generous friends had given us and toasted to our new beginning as a couple. That is all of the play-by-play that you will get because, don't forget, I had been sleeping on Hannah's couch for the past six weeks!

The next morning I loaded all of the luggage and gear that was, thanks to Hannah, neatly organized and placed by the front door, and we headed west. We had done a little research and found a house rental in Oceanside, California, just a block from the beach, and a cabin in the northern mountains of Arizona. This gave us a few days on the beach with ocean air and a few days of playing in the snow. The energy and excitement of all of this made me very emotional many times. I thought that this 55-year- old was going to grow old by himself and here I was, sitting next to my wife whose smile was as real and big as mine.

Hannah

As I sat in the car gazing out the window, I was reflecting on all of the losses I had suffered over the past few years. God called each one to mind and showed me that he had restored them all by giving me Chuck in my life. I now had a new home with him. I had a new marriage, a new vocation, and a new best friend. Chuck was also my health coach-- helping me to juice, exercise regularly, and keep my dreams alive. It truly stunned me when God showed me how He had restored all of those losses. It became a daily reminder to me that God sees me and loves me, and all of the details of life.

We had packed our bikes along for our honeymoon. Our mutual love for biking made our time in California so much fun. We adventured down the coast for seventeen miles on our bikes and took the train home, exploring beaches and restaurants while breathing in the fresh salty breezes. We stood knee-deep in the ocean water, arm in arm praying. We met all sorts of people who got to hear our amazing God stories.

Now it wasn't just Chuck's story. I had become an amazing part of his story, and he of mine. Every time we mentioned to a restaurant server that we were on our honeymoon, we were gifted some kind of dessert! We just laughed about it after the 4th time it happened and were just really glad we were biking everywhere to help burn off all the extra calories. We spent hours watching sunsets and dreaming aloud of our future.

We walked hand in hand on the beach. It was idyllic, like a fairytale. These were the beautiful moments in which Chuck promised me that our honeymoon would never be over. This vow meant so much to me, having experienced abandonment and rejection. It was a pledge that I knew was authentic and real, and one I would need to keep hearing over and over for the rest of what would become a challenging year. We would continue to repeat that to each other almost daily, especially when something difficult would happen.

Chuck

After a few days at the beach going for walks and riding bikes, the sun started tanning our bodies. We rode bikes that evening down to a sushi place, went inside, and were shown to our table. I reached out for Hannah's hand like I still do at dinner, looked her in the eyes, and then looked at her nose. I never saw Hannah with a tan and her nose had browned up and it was the cutest thing I had ever seen. I couldn't shut up about it and she just laughed because it was the first time I'd seen her with a tan. It was a great reminder of how new this all was and I absolutely loved it!

We both love the beach and the ocean air, but we talked about our second love for the mountains, pines, and snow. So according to plan after five days in beautiful California, we packed up and headed east to our next stop, which was just south of Flagstaff. When we drove up to our rented cabin there were ten inches of snow on the porch. We went from the sun and the sand to the mountains and snow in just a few hours. And since you can't go to the snow without building a snowman and making snow angels, Hannah's joy in those moments made something come alive in me that I never experienced before—love, trust, and knowing that if one of us was on a ledge, the other one would be there without a doubt to make the catch.

After three days playing in the snow, we drove forty-five minutes south to beautiful Sedona, which is on the way home to Phoenix. We absolutely love the beauty of the red rock formations. Our first hike was up Bell Rock. If you have not seen it before, it is very unique and just as beautiful. We actually hiked the highest I have ever been on Bell Rock and then sat down side by side to enjoy the breathtaking view. One of the things I pointed out to Hannah was the Chapel of the Holy Cross. It's a church that an architect designed back in the 50's that sits on the side of a rock formation. I told Hannah we were headed there next. We hiked down after meeting some new friends and telling them our story.

We drove over and parked at the Holy Chapel. Maybe it's just me, but I always feel the energy of the Holy Spirit when I'm around it. Hannah and I went in and kneeled down in the front row. You can see the Sedona valley out through the windows and there is a statue of Jesus on the cross the entire size of the front of the church. I had so much to thank Him for and as soon as I started praying the tears started rolling. If you have never experienced a situation where you can feel the love of God holding you that tightly, I pray that you do. As I finished praying and I opened my eyes and looked over at Hannah—this beautiful person I just made a commitment to for the rest of my life—I saw she also had tears rolling down her face from her chat with God. What more could a guy ask for?

Hannah

Once we got back home to Phoenix, we quickly fell into our routines of housework, organizing Chuck's stuff into the closets, and figuring out our next steps as a married couple. Chuck had several landscaping and irrigation jobs lined up and I decided to tag along and learn how he did his work. It was another peek into who Chuck was and how he interacted with his clients. Every job became an opportunity for him to share his testimony. Every trip to Home Depot to buy parts was a chance for him to make another connection. He had more than enough work, but we could sense that we needed to make time and space for our new calling. We kept talking about starting a nonprofit. We watched multiple YouTube videos, read articles, and Googled the basic steps. We knew we had two options: hire an attorney to get things started or do the work ourselves. We quickly realized that a lawyer was out of the question. Their fees were $5,000-$7,000 and that was money we didn't have. So we did our homework and prayed a lot. Just one week after returning home from our honeymoon and having pushed our desks together to create a home office, we applied for our official nonprofit name. We had been praying and brainstorming a name, and God just dropped "Living Hope Cancer Foundation" into our spirits. It was perfect. It was both a name of God and the very thing we desired for every cancer patient: to live with hope.

As we continued to research the steps, we prayed over every page of paperwork and submitted the final draft on January 28, 2020, just a few weeks after our wedding. From everything we had seen, we assumed it would take 4-6 months to get a reply from the IRS, whether it was positive or negative. Meanwhile, we continued with our coaching calls and messages and began planning to build a website.

Our January schedule was packed. Chuck had previously committed to be the keynote speaker for an American Cancer Society (ACS) 2020 kickoff, and he also had rescheduled his trip to Traverse City, Michigan. The ACS event gave me my first glimpse into how Chuck operated in front of a crowd. Until then, I had only watched a YouTube video of him on stage telling his story. This was something different. Something I could get used to. Listening to his dynamic story just never got old. Four months of hearing it on a regular basis (often daily) was helping *me* learn how to tell it. And now we had to learn how to add my story into it. This was our first public opportunity as a united front, as a married couple. Little did we know that this was just God's trial run for us. Soon He would be placing us in front of groups and crowds all over the country. We would both become published authors and share our stories in person, via social media, and on stage.

But we couldn't learn how to do that without the smaller steps of practicing on people in coffee shops, in the airport, in the park, and on the street.

God was leading us to speak to the people around us at every opportune moment.

And that is exactly what we did.

Chuck

Figuring out how to do life with Hannah was exciting, fun, and way easier than I had ever imagined. Boy, did I meet my match. Beautiful, smart, and with strong work ethics? After my cancer miracle, I called myself the most blessed guy in the world, and now it was happening again with Hannah! One of my first commitments after our wedding was taking my rescheduled trip to Traverse City. I was going there to visit Jay Desantis, whom I met through a buddy from my hometown that was now working in Michigan. He had heard about someone recently diagnosed with Stage 4 pancreatic cancer. My buddy suggested without hesitation, "He has to meet Chuck. He's a Stage 4 survivor with a miraculous story." I was introduced to Jay, his wife, and their son over the phone and not only was I coaching the positive mindset through cancer, but I was also praying with them. We had formed a bond, just like family. I started preparing myself for a trip across the country to spend three days with them.

After I landed in Traverse City and walked up to Jay, who I had never met in person, you would think we had grown up together. His wife and son were so amazing and made me feel at home. We talked about how to get the most out of a life with a cancer diagnosis. We hiked in the snow overlooking Lake Michigan and the time flew by. In between, I was FaceTiming with my new bride and missing her. I poured my heart out while I was there to make sure when I left that Jay and his family were going to be okay no matter what came their way. I flew back to Phoenix mentally and physically exhausted. I landed around close to midnight and dragged my tired self through the airport so I could head to the car and go home. But then I looked up and I saw something that to me was the closest thing to an angel as you can get. Walking towards me was my beautiful wife with my pup Jax on the leash next to her and I thought I died and went to heaven. I wasn't used to having someone to come home to. God blessed me with feelings I never got to feel before.

The honeymoon is *never* over!

CHAPTER TEN

Blind Faith

Hannah

The week after Chuck's trip to Michigan (we decided there were no more trips apart after that!), we had two speaking engagements on our schedule. The first one was for a high school class at a local charter school. The classroom was packed full of about seventy-five 17-year-olds. We took turns sharing our stories and at one point Chuck asked the class, "How many of you know someone affected by cancer?" Nearly the entire class raised their hands.

Since it was a public school, we were asked not to talk about our faith, but it's pretty hard to tell a miracle story about Jesus touching you without mentioning Jesus. The kids had tears running down their faces and were visibly moved. The teacher said, "I have never seen my students so quiet and focused at one time." We were learning how powerful our story was for any age group.

Chuck

The next day, I was invited to speak at the Rotary Club in Tempe. The event started with breakfast and we met some amazing people, including a gentleman who was working on one of the islands where they were testing nuclear bombs. He's also an author, and he gave us a copy of his book. It's interesting that whether I'm on stage speaking to a large group or if I'm just talking to someone in the park while walking Jax, the story is always the same. The group that morning was very warm and we shared hugs and handshakes before we left. I think it was at that moment, I realized our story was changing. First, it was my miracle story, then it was how my miracle story changed me, and now it's the miracle story that includes a lot of lessons and learning how God has blessed me with a new wife. Adding Hannah's amazing journey about her challenges and cancer and how together we are dealing with everything truly is the beginning of a new story.

Hannah

The next month flew by as we had our first board meeting for our nonprofit and had meetings with multiple people. We introduced each other to several of our visiting friends and family and met with local coaching clients over coffee or a meal. I went to my usual doctor visits, but instead of just going alone as I had done for the past three years, Chuck came along for support and to keep me company. We did everyday life together and we loved it. Our schedules were packed full every week.

The highlight was Valentine's Day. We had been invited to be interviewed by our local Fox News affiliate. This was our first time on TV together, and we didn't know what to expect. The crew arrived at our house with video cameras, lights, and clip-on microphones. The reporter asked us questions for thirty minutes straight and we just talked and talked. We both love sharing our amazing love story of getting married in mid-life after both being diagnosed with Stage 4 cancer. Our love story was set to run on their TV station early the next day as their Valentine's Day Special. We watched with anticipation. They showed a clip from our wedding video of us biking home on our tandem, and several short clips of us speaking—all of which was summed up in ninety seconds! It was amazing how they had condensed thirty minutes of conversation into just one and a half minutes of content. The news reporter summarized our story by titling it a "Divine Pairing." It struck us that she had used those words and recognized the significance of the fact that God had brought the two of us together.

We had another speaking engagement lined up at the Phoenix Art Museum on the evening of Valentine's Day. Our dear friend Kanu had a podcast called *Real Love Real Stories*. She had collaborated with the museum to put on an event that night to share local "love stories" and had invited us to speak. It was another opportunity to speak our story out loud. I definitely needed the practice! The more I told it, the more relaxed I was and the easier it became.

The rest of the month was full of more doctor's appointments, a CT scan, natural IV infusions, and lymphatic massage. This was my life as a Stage 4 cancer patient in active treatment. My breast cancer was stable which meant it was not growing and remained the same in some of the lymph nodes in both the lungs and my armpit. I was on a daily oral pill, a form of chemotherapy. My biggest complaint was fatigue, a symptom that I learned to push through when needed and to rest when I could. I always gave myself nine hours of rest at night, which helped my energy level during the day. Chuck had observed me for months and noticed exactly when I needed to take a break. I wasn't used to sharing the housework or having someone pick up the slack, so it was amazing to me when he got the vacuum cleaner out and had the dishwasher emptied before I got out of bed! I had married a man with skills! "Acts of service" is my love language and he was speaking his love to me, loud and clear.

Chuck

I was first introduced to Pastor Mark Rush a year or so earlier as he traveled on his journey with brain cancer. I spent long hours on the phone with Mark and was so moved by his contentment with life that we asked him to sit on the board of directors for our foundation. Hannah and I were able to get to know Mark and his wife Gretchen via video chats and they invited us to visit them on their ranch in Texas. Around the same time, we were presented with an opportunity to visit Franklin, Tennessee, through a seemingly random event. But we know it was really God's plan.

Hannah

I have been part of a Christian Medical Share plan for many years and they 100% reimbursed my natural IV infusion treatments. A month after being diagnosed with cancer, I began receiving high doses of Vitamin C and many other vitamins and minerals to support my immune system while also doing conventional cancer treatment. The reimbursement method was accomplished by submitting the bills and then the company allocated specific dollar amounts to the various members which then would be directly sent to me.

This particular month, I opened my mailbox and found a check with a letter from a man named Ben. He wrote in his letter that he normally never wrote letters but felt that God had told him to write to me and offer to pray with me. We set up a time together and made the call. Ben told us that he was living in the Franklin, Tennessee area and was starting a ministry there. After praying a beautiful prayer of healing over me, he invited us to a Spirit-Led Conference in March. I immediately just *knew* that we were supposed to attend.

As we began discussing a potential trip to Tennessee, it made sense to first travel to Texas to visit Mark, continue on to Franklin, and then pop up to Ohio to see Chuck's parents.

Chuck

One afternoon, we were sitting outside together enjoying the sunshine and perfect temperatures of a late February day in Phoenix. Hannah got up from her chair and walked down the driveway to the mailbox. As I looked up from my phone, she had a funny look on her face and had her arm outstretched towards me, holding a letter.

"You open it," she said nervously.

As I looked at the return address, I could see that it was from the IRS. I ripped open the envelope and unfolded the paper. "Dear Applicant," it began, "We are pleased to tell you we determined you're exempt from the Federal Income Tax."

We had received our 501(c)3 tax exemption status in just 4 short weeks!

It was official. We were a legitimate nonprofit. This would allow individuals to support our work with cancer patients and their families by donating money and receiving a tax write-off. This was a huge benefit for us since all of our expenses for travel, building a website, covering Zoom expenses for conference calls, etc., had all been coming out of our own pockets. We were slightly shocked at how quickly it had been granted and immediately recognized God's favor on us. We had asked Him for big things and He said, "You have not seen anything yet." It was just the beginning.

If you would have told me a few short years ago I would soon be a Stage 4 cancer survivor, would dedicate my life to Jesus, would be married to the girl of my dreams, would be the co-founder of a cancer foundation, and would be coaching and loving on cancer patients and their families every day, I would have laughed and told you that you'd lost your mind. But this is how God works. Let go and let God. No really, let go.

CHAPTER ELEVEN

Texas, Tennessee, and Road Trips

Hannah

Hand in hand we crossed over the threshold of the plane. It was our first official "business trip" for Living Hope Cancer Foundation. We were armed with a hundred or so silicone bracelets that we had designed and printed that we could hand out as "business cards" to anyone we met, whether at the airport, sitting next to us on the plane, or in a coffee shop. We passed them out as if they were candy. They became an amazing way to break the ice and share our miracle stories. Now our audiences had a way to reach us. We had a website, a logo, a mission statement, and a whole lot of purpose. We knew that God was steering this ship and we saw Him at work in all of the details of our plans. Whether it was lodging, or transportation, or finances, He was providing and guiding us along the way.

We arrived in Houston, Texas, very excited to meet Mark (our friend with brain cancer) and Gretchen Rush. They had recommended that we rent a car for the one-and-a-half-hour drive to their ranch. As we approached the rental counter, we were helped by a lovely woman who was all smiles. As we began to share our story, she told us she also had a family member with cancer. It was God's way of showing us that we were on the right path of coaching people. We were beginning to notice that everywhere we went and opened our hearts and mouths, the blessings would pour out.

I had overheard Chuck joking with Mark over the phone and he said, "I hope you have a couch for Hannah and me to crash on because we are getting too old to sleep on the floor." We didn't need to worry. We pulled up to our friend's property and were amazed at the view. It was an 80-acre Texas ranch and they provided us with our own tiny cabin, one of five, built for their nonprofit ministry which served to help restore marriages.

So our accommodations were a private log cabin on a lake. It was like our second honeymoon! I guess we *had* declared that our honeymoon would never be over. We came to serve them and ended up being fed, housed, and encouraged *by* them. We spent our mornings wandering around the little town meeting all kinds of people, passing out bracelets and hope. Everywhere we went, we met people with cancer stories of their own or of a family member, including ladies crocheting prayer blankets, a coffee shop owner, and a random woman on the sidewalk. Cancer knows no boundaries and we were beginning to *really* see the value of the job that God had given us.

Chuck

The next stop on this three-city tour was Franklin, Tennessee, just outside of Nashville. And we discovered so many coincidences before we landed that I looked up at the sky and thanked God. Before we arrived, three different friends told me that they had close friends in the area that we needed to meet.

As our plane finally descended toward Nashville, Hannah, who was sitting three rows in front of me, stood up, turned around, and let me know her book was just published. We both shouted out in celebration because we knew how hard Hannah and her team had worked on the book. Finally, everyone could learn more about her journey overcoming huge hurdles in life through the new paperback called, **Faith Like Skin**. Everyone who knows Hannah knows the title was not a catchy one just to sell books; it is truly how Hannah lives her life every day.

Through our tours and planned events, it's easy to imagine how we can touch others and try to change lives. But there's more to the story. The people we meet outside of those formal events in airports, hotels, and restaurants are also part of it. When someone shares with us what they or a loved one is going through, we get to pray with them wherever we are, whether in the middle of a crowded airport or a huddle-up in a store. Praying and tears flowing have become a daily part of our lives.

While in Franklin, we decided to visit financial expert Dave Ramsey's office and radio production studio. When you walk into this brand new building, you're greeted with a sign saying: "Remember, there's ultimately only one way to financial peace and that's to walk daily with the Prince of Peace, Christ Jesus." I heard that you have to tell your God story on your application for employment. The staff there is amazing. When we started telling them about our cancer journey, they went wild. We got to share and pray with so many. We even got to meet Dave and some of his staff and after three hours of high-energy conversations, we needed to go home and take a nap.

Not long after arriving in Tennessee, we got a pleasant surprise that my Ohio high school buddy Joe and his fiancee, Tami, were making the drive to meet us. We were excited to see them. And since the cost of the airline ticket from Tennessee to our next stop in Ohio had doubled overnight, Joe and Tami let us ride with them back to Columbus the next day. Without a doubt, it was God's plan.

The event in Franklin was a Spirit-driven conference. Although a new concept for me, I was excited to learn more about how it could help me improve my faith. The main speaker was a guy named Ravi. He was featured in a documentary, *Father of Lights*, where he would hear God giving him instructions in his dreams and the events would happen just the way he was told. Ravi blew us away when we had a chance to speak with him. He told us that he dreamed that he was going to speak at this event and meet Hannah and me. And that dream had come eleven years earlier. Although it sounds crazy, I believe God has messengers and we have heard so many prophetic words and instructions. Ravi told us that as Living Hope Cancer Foundation grows, that it will change from Hannah and me traveling around the country, to having a place where people will come to us. He said we will own some acreage and buildings. It wouldn't be 11 acres, but just under that amount, "10 point something." Hannah and I looked at each other in amazement not knowing what to think. We don't know if this will come true or not, but it caused us to think about our future in a new way.

Hannah

After amazing conversations in the car with Joe and Tami, we arrived in Ohio. I didn't realize that we were building relationships with them for future events. (I should have figured that out! God was guiding every single step of our lives and He had a purpose for every relationship.)

As we settled in to stay a few nights with Chuck's brother, Tony, we made plans to see his parents and visit the Arthur G. James Cancer Hospital at The Ohio State University. But while climbing the stairs to the bedroom that first night, I felt super winded and could barely catch my breath. I chalked it up to not being used to stairs since our home is on one floor. The next day we decided to walk around town to grab breakfast and visit the cancer center. As we got closer to about our second mile of walking, I started to get dizzy and had to bend over to catch my breath. My heart was pounding and I felt awful. *What is going on?* I thought to myself. Chuck was very patient as we made our way to the building, and I was able to rest a bit before we met a few people that Chuck knew. They introduced us to their colleagues that had all read Chuck's book and we handed out more of our bracelets. Our dream is to partner with cancer centers all over the country so we can become that missing "next room" after someone is diagnosed with cancer and is scared and confused.

We finally arrived back home to Arizona full of ideas, amazing experiences, and new dreams to explore. We were beginning to see the path God was showing us to follow. We knew that we had to continue to work hard, one day at a time, but now we had a clearer direction, a better vision with end goals that served more people effectively. This platform was way bigger than we had imagined!

Chuck

Our faith was growing just like everything else around us. Can you imagine a life where God orchestrates everything? Of course, not everything happens immediately because God knows you can't drop someone into something they can't handle. So far, we had experienced lots of lessons and signals and were learning how to *get up and live* to put these lessons into action. Talking to one person at the gym, or in the park while walking Jax or to someone at the grocery store told us how powerful our story was and what others found to be the most important. All of this helped us prepare for standing on stage at churches, businesses, and schools. We've been going through God school. And that first trip as Living Hope Cancer Foundation was one of many amazing things we nurtured and developed. I used to say I was lucky, but I don't believe in luck anymore. I believe God already had this planned and blesses us on good days and tough days.

CHAPTER TWELVE

For Better or for Worse

Hannah

The elevated heart rate I first experienced in Ohio gave me concern. This was new and different and I needed answers. I scheduled a visit with a cardiologist a few days after we got home from our trip. He couldn't see any immediate issues and suggested we monitor my heart for the next two weeks. The results were inconclusive. My echocardiogram was clear. He had no answers for me. Since I also had some breathing difficulties, the next doctor I was sent to was a pulmonologist, exactly one month later. Again, they couldn't give me an answer. I had some breathing trouble but they were unable to pinpoint the cause. By now it was mid-April of 2020 and the world was in full pandemic mode as we scrounged for toilet paper, sewed masks, and "Zoomed" our way through work and birthday parties. To avoid spiking my heart rate or losing my breath, we found a used tandem bike and I was able to pedal along. My goal was to keep moving even if I was uncomfortable. And if I couldn't bike on my own, I could be on the back of a bike. I was determined.

Soon after that, I also started having issues with my back and neck and needed Chuck to regularly massage those areas. I thought perhaps I had slept on my neck wrong or pulled a muscle. The one thing that made it feel better was if I asked him to gently pull my head up and off my neck. That stretch gave me instant relief.

I was finally able to see my oncologist to discuss my changing health status. Now up until this point, I had been continuing to take the oral pills that stabilized my cancer. This meeting was the very first of many Telemed calls I would have. I'd never Facetimed a doctor before. I found it very convenient. He suggested that we do another CT scan to see if we could find an answer.

With all the new aches and pains and annoying physical changes, it never even crossed my mind that it could be cancer spreading. I was caught up with the joys and busyness of being a newlywed and a co-founder of a newly started non-profit organization. It didn't fit in *my* plans to have to navigate progressing cancer, especially the type of breast cancer I would soon be diagnosed with.

The scans showed that there was a tumor in a lymph node sitting on my pulmonary artery and airway. It was causing both elevated heart rate symptoms and shortness of breath. There was also some new activity in several nodes in my chest, lungs, armpits, liver, and a spot in my groin on the bone. This was a significant spread. My oncologist was calm but firm about my needing to pursue a new treatment. He already knew about my past hesitation regarding radiation and intravenous chemotherapy. He set up a meeting for me with a radiation oncologist the next day.

Was I scared? Yes. Did Chuck and I cry in each other's arms? Definitely. But we reminded each other that these test results weren't a surprise to God, that God promised to be with us and never leave us, and that we weren't alone. This time my response to "bad cancer news" was different. I wasn't reacting out of desperation. I had confidence in knowing that whatever God allowed in my life had a purpose. He wasn't *causing* the cancer. We blame the hard stuff on Satan.

Looking back, I see how this could have easily unseated both of us and our new foundation, a ministry designed to serve and love people. It's exactly what the enemy hates and seeks to destroy. I was beginning to learn and see how God had a purpose for my pain. Up till now, it had been mostly emotional pain.

Then one Saturday morning I woke up in complete physical pain.

The day before, I had been shocked when the radiation oncologist pointed out an image from the CT scan of a tumor in the C5 vertebrae in my neck. This was more news we were not expecting. It explained the nagging discomfort I had been dealing with in my neck and shoulders. But now we had a game plan based on scans and tests. Early the next week, I would be mapped for radiation and receive my first round. I also had a liver biopsy scheduled to determine the type of cancer. They would also start my chemo treatment around the same time. The treatment needed to start as soon as possible. There was no time to lose.

But I wasn't able to move forward in my treatment plan. The next day, the pain soon became so intense that I woke up in agony and began vomiting. Chuck quickly packed me into his truck and drove me to the Emergency Room. We were very aware that I would have to traverse this next part of my journey into the hospital alone due to COVID restrictions that were in place. We were a mere month and a half into the pandemic and the "drop off at the door" policy was in full effect.

A nurse brought me a wheelchair, took my temperature, and made me say goodbye to my husband before she whisked me into the corridor. It was so eerie. The waiting room was blocked off and dark. I was checked in from the hallway and then brought to a small dark room. I carefully climbed onto the stretcher and laid down. No extra sounds were echoing through the hallways that I had come to expect from the Emergency Room. No beeps or alarms. No voices chattering in conversations. No overhead sound speaker. Nothing. The hospital was largely empty. People were staying home to avoid getting COVID. Fewer people also meant less staff. I was left alone. All alone. Vomiting. Experiencing the most intense pain (besides natural childbirth) I had ever felt. I was miserable and all I could do was cry out to Jesus.

The orderly came to take me for a CT scan. Not much later, a doctor came into the room, sat down, and explained to me that my neck was broken at the C5 level. I thought to myself, *Who walks around with a broken neck?* Now I was like Chuck who at one point walked around with a fractured spine.

The doctor seemed to indicate that this was a very serious situation I was in. The staff immediately placed a brace around my neck to stabilize it from further damage. The physical movement of vomiting had not helped my fracture and had possibly caused it! The ER doctor was reaching out to another hospital that was equipped to perform neck surgery and started discussing the need to transfer me as soon as possible for surgery.

I could barely keep up. All of this information was overwhelming and completely unexpected. I had been thinking that I was going to receive radiation the following week to address the neck tumor (and that thought was bad enough!) and now I was going to have neck surgery? The nurse was aware that Chuck was camping out in the ER parking lot just to stay close by to me.

Chuck

The only thing I knew while sitting in that parking lot was Hannah was in agonizing pain that was increasing and I was not going to leave. I laid down in the back of my truck, snapped a selfie, and sent it to Hannah. A few minutes went by and my beautiful newlywed wife sent back a selfie from the ER in a hospital. At this point, the only thing I could do is pray and hold back the tears. A couple of hours slowly went by as we were waiting for answers and a game plan.

Out of nowhere, I jumped when there was a knock on my truck window. It was a nurse from the ER. She said they were getting test results back slowly and the results were not good. Hannah had a fracture in her C5 vertebrae. Somewhere in the past 24 hours, her neck had broken. I could tell by the look on her face she was scared and this was very serious. She asked me to follow her. I asked her, "Where to?"

Since it was May of 2020 and security guards were stationed at hospital entrances because of Covid; there was no gaining entrance. But she handed me a mask and let me know she was going to sneak me through another door so I could be with my wife. Time stopped, my body went numb, and my heart sank as I followed this messenger down a hallway and into a room. Hannah lay there all covered up and now wearing a neck brace. We think the violent vomiting from the pain caused a small fracture in her spine to grow into a massive compression fracture. Either way, they were getting ready to transport her to another hospital for emergency surgery.

The feeling I got was they allowed me to break the rules and enter the hospital during Covid because they did not know when I would see her again or *if* I would see her again. A couple of hours went by as we sat there holding hands. Then the nurse came in and said her transport was there. I followed along as they wheeled

Hannah outside to the ambulance and I stood there and watched as they loaded her in, shut the doors, and turned on the flashing lights, and drove off.

CHAPTER THIRTEEN

Tubie

Hannah

Surreal is the best word I can come up with to describe the situation that I found myself in. I was loaded into an ambulance in the middle of the night when I should have been home and safely tucked in my bed next to my new husband. Instead, I found myself being transported through the dark corridors of a hospital strapped to a stretcher, turn after turn through empty hallways until at last, I arrived in a bright little room bustling with staff.

The nurses very carefully moved me to the bed in the room and immediately I felt a warm wet shower cap fitted onto my head. The girl at the head of the bed began to gently massage my scalp. I realized that the cap was full of suds and water and that she was actually washing my long brown curly hair.

It was completely unexpected and felt strangely luxurious, something I would expect in a spa and not a hospital room. Maybe this was a perk of Covid with fewer patients in the hospital and enough staff to serve the patients. It was an odd comfort in an otherwise very uncomfortable situation and one that I welcomed wholeheartedly. It was a God wink. He was reminding me He was with me in *this* hard thing too.

Early Monday morning I was transported to the pre-op area. A very strange-looking astronaut-like suited man approached me. I realized that this was my anesthesiologist protecting himself from possible Covid contamination. After all, he was the most exposed person in the operating room when he intubated a patient. I felt like I was in a sci-fi movie. Everything moved in slow motion as I signed the consent form to have the first of two surgeries performed on my neck in two days. They needed to cut off the blood supply to the tumor in my neck and the only way to do that was to cut off the right cerebral artery. After hearing the horrifying possible side effects, I signed my life away.

The following day would be the neck fusion. It was explained to me that the surgeon would operate through the front of my neck and remove the tumor while rebuilding the space with bone putty and stabilizing the area with titanium rods and screws. I woke up in the Neuro ICU all alone. The pain was manageable with narcotics and I was fitted with a brace to wear at home for the following 7 weeks. Initially, I needed to wear this brace 24/7, even while sleeping. It was the weirdest feeling to have a fabric-covered piece of plastic velcroed around my neck. It also felt incredibly strange to *not* have the brace fastened around my neck. The area was incredibly unstable and weak.

I spent those days in the Intensive Care Unit flat on my back. The only thing I could do was to turn on the worship playlist on my phone and blast the music. The song *The Blessing* had just been released by Elevation Music and I recall laying with my arms raised in worship with tears pouring down my face. The nurse came in during one of these holy moments, respecting my need to cry and sing. I'd just survived one of the hardest moments of my life. I was both fearless and bold to share my faith with anyone that walked in the room. I was starting to notice that the more "Hard Places" I was visiting in my cancer journey, the less I cared about how others perceived my faith journey. This was between me and God. That ICU was simultaneously the loneliest I had felt (practically abandoned by the staff due to Covid) and the closest I had ever felt to God. It was like He was sitting on the bed with me. That close!

Chuck

I was spending a lot of my time either waiting for a call or text from Hannah or a call from one of the many doctors. The mental aspect of what I had just watched my wife go through was definitely challenging my faith. The devil tried to step in and throw all of the what-ifs at me, but I kept going to God for strength to keep my sanity. I was thinking I would be hearing from Hannah off and on for updates over the next few days to say hi and to see how she was doing. For any of you who know Hannah, there is always room for surprise and change. I decided now was not the time for an exception. I was prepared to pick her up in three to five days and get her home to her comfortable bed. After hitting the gym, I ran by the grocery store. I figured I would get the house cleaned up later that day or tomorrow. I was taking some cancer coaching calls for the foundation when the phone rang and I did not know the number that came up. I picked it up and it was Hannah on a hospital phone. I was excited to hear her voice. We had not spoken much the day before because of the surgery.

I said, "Hi baby, how are you feeling?"

She responded, "I feel pretty good. They are going to release me and I want you to be ready to come to get me."

"Ummmm. Wait a minute. You are in the ICU," I replied.

"I know," she said, "The doctor said I can come home. It will be easier to rest in my own bed."

Most people go from surgery to ICU so the nurses can keep a close eye on them. Once everything is okay in a day or two, then they're moved to a regular room to recover. But not Hannah! Two hours later I was pulling up at the hospital's patient release door and a nurse came out pushing Hannah in a wheelchair. We loaded her into the car. I got her home safely and into the comfort of her big cozy bed. It made me think a lot about my own journey with Stage 4 cancer only five years earlier. In a number of situations during that time, I made up my mind to push forward, to *get up and live*, to go against what doctors and family were saying. Now Hannah was doing that exact same thing.

Hannah

We settled into a routine at home of eating soft mushy foods (since the surgery had been through the front of my neck and I couldn't swallow anything hard or crunchy), enjoying our mornings outside in the rocking chairs, and afternoons on the couch resting.

A week after returning home from the hospital, I started radiation on the tumor that was sitting on the pulmonary artery. The plan was to have ten radiation treatments in a row which occurred on Monday to Friday with weekends off. They were roughly about the same time every day, in the early afternoon, lasting about ten minutes with only about two minutes on the table. I felt like I was in an episode of "Lost." The machine looked like a model from the 1960s. The technician had me lay on a hard table with a pillow under my knees. The machine rotated around me with red laser lights to measure its precision, then there would be a series of clicks and beeps before a long clanging sound to indicate the radiation beam was being applied—in my case, once on the back and once on the front of my body. About 2-3 hours after the treatment each day, which usually was around dinner time, I would experience severe fatigue making me want to faceplant into my dinner plate.

I was simultaneously receiving intravenous chemotherapy once a week. Radiation and chemotherapy are usually not given at the same time. It was an indication of how concerned my oncologists were with the progression of cancer in my body. By the second treatment, my head started itching and getting sore. I had read enough breast cancer support group conversations to know that it was time to get a big haircut. I had long curly hair down my back and did not want to experience hair loss with long locks of hair falling out. That felt like it would be traumatic. I'm a firm believer in controlling what I *can* control. It's not often when you can wear a mohawk at age 46. I decided to get a "momhawk." The hairdresser shaved the sides of my head and left a cute middle section that I scrunched up into curls. I had some semblance of control and I knew it wouldn't be as difficult to shave my head when it came time.

I was having increasing difficulties swallowing food. I was admitted into the hospital in late May, just two weeks after surgery. The medical staff could not identify the cause and sent me home. Two more times I went to the ER with severe swallowing issues and no diagnosis. These were long, lonely hours of being left entirely alone because of staff restrictions due to Covid. Finally, I was admitted again in early June, completely unable to swallow my own saliva. I was spitting in a cup. Everything hurt. I was dehydrated. The staff inserted IVs and brought me up to my room. It took three days and several scans to figure out that I had severe ulcerations in my esophagus related to radiation. All this time, the doctors were citing the neck surgery as the cause since the entrance wound was in the front of my neck. Now we had answers and the only solution to stay alive was to have a feeding tube inserted through my stomach. It felt extreme but I had lost 15 pounds in three weeks and was losing strength. I underwent yet another surgery to have the feeding tube inserted.

Five days after being admitted, I was reunited with Chuck. Armed with instructions on how to feed myself using the tube, I happily returned home. I had to pour everything that I would normally swallow into the feeding tube which was a huge syringe attached to a small catheter. We bought organic specially-balanced nutrition shakes to help me regain my strength and serve as my daily food intake. There was a bit of a learning curve, even though I was a nurse. I had never touched a feeding tube before. I had to change the dressing daily. I would feed myself every two hours along with water and pulverized medicine mixed with liquid. I affectionately named the feeding tube, "Tubie."

I wasn't able to eat by mouth for several weeks. Being a "foodie," it was not easy. I love food. I love cooking. I felt like both of these things had been taken from me. But I recognized that it was a season. It wouldn't be forever even if the enemy was whispering that in my ear and trying to make me falter in my faith. I was learning to let the losses and the lessons of those losses teach me to take them to God. He knew how much I loved food. And maybe that was exactly it. Maybe I needed to hold the stuff of this world a little more loosely. Maybe I needed to have a more grateful heart for each morsel I had been taking for granted and had just been shoveling in my face. I now had an entirely new perspective on food—one that I wouldn't forget too quickly. Sometimes you don't miss it, or realize its value, till it's gone.

CHAPTER FOURTEEN

I'm a Lifer

Chuck

With Hannah going through all of these physical and mental challenges, I knew it was my job as her husband and caregiver to make her as comfortable as possible. Being a caregiver is absolutely exhausting. Not only are you concerned about taking care of your loved one's every need, but you are also going through the situation with them as well. Our situation was caused by cancer, but many experience it because of other diagnoses or even a car accident. The caregiver feels it all and gives and gives. I found myself needing to think *mind over matter*, a lot like how things were during my own cancer journey. I decided as long as I was Hannah's caregiver, and as tough as it was, I wanted to be the number one caregiver in the world. You can ask Hannah. I was, and still am, going for it!

Along the way, I asked a few of my neighbors if anyone had a wheelchair. One of my friends said he had one in his garage and I was welcome to use it. I took it home and shined it all up. Boy, did I have a big surprise for Hannah. "Can you come outside?" I asked her. "I want to show you something."

She held onto my arm as we slowly worked our way out to the front driveway one baby step at a time and there it was. I was so excited to show her this wheelchair! But when I looked back at her face, tears were rolling down her cheeks. When I asked her what was wrong, she told me she wasn't getting into that thing and there was no way she wanted to be seen in a wheelchair. *What?* I thought she would be excited. So I looked into her eyes and told her that if she didn't get into the chair, there would be no way for us to get to the end of the street to watch the sunset.

A few minutes went by while Hannah decided to swallow her pride. This was an unexpected hurdle. Something that I thought would be a happy surprise ended up being a thinking moment. Finally, she looked at me and told me I was right, and got into the chair. She could have said no, but sunset with her hubby was special. But then something else happened. Since she disliked the wheelchair so much and had no intention of staying in it very long, it became her motivation to get better as quickly as possible. She did not want to have it symbolize that she was losing her independence. After only a few trips, Hannah asked me to push her some and she then walked some. Only two weeks later, the wheelchair was sitting at home and Hannah was walking around the block with Jax and me. And soon, she was walking a mile.

The next challenge was dealing with the new chemo that was going to make Hannah's hair fall out. Hannah had 14 inches of beautiful dark wavy hair, so we knew it would be an issue. Hannah told me she had a friend who cuts hair, so we called her and set up an appointment. The thought was to get a chic short haircut so we could ease into her ongoing hair loss. Hannah looked cute in her new hairdo, but within just a few weeks her hair started falling out in clumps. We knew the next step was to shave it off. What an emotional experience for both of us. We cried and hugged as I set up a chair and got out the hair trimmers.

I always document experiences in our journey, so I set up my phone and did a timelapse video. It started with me shaving Hannah's hair completely off, and then I handed her the trimmer. She tried to talk me out of shaving my head for no reason, but I was in full support mode and I wanted her to know that we were in this together, every step of the way. To show people our love and bond, I posted the video on social media and watched as nearly 20,000 people shared in that special moment.

With the surgeries and the extensive treatments, I never let myself get too far from Hannah. I even stopped going to the gym because I could not leave her home alone. While she lost 20 pounds when she couldn't swallow solid food, my temporary change of lifestyle resulted in me somehow gaining it.

Hannah

Being bald was new to me since this was my first experience with intravenous chemotherapy. I thought I would be devastated losing my hair, but I found it oddly liberating. I'd learned to look for the silver linings over the past few years, each time I went through a loss. The good news is I didn't have to worry about bad hair days and I saved time getting ready in the mornings. I started making and finding extra large dangling earrings and playing with my makeup.

A new thing I experienced was that people noticed my baldness and almost immediately could identify that I had cancer. Even though I had already been on my cancer journey for three years, no one ever knew it. It felt strange to have my diagnosis "out there" for everyone to see. I was beginning to experience some of the feelings and emotions that my cancer coaching clients went through—stuff I would never have understood had I not been able to journey through it myself.

Chuck's unending support bolstered my drive to stay active. He would look me in the eyes when I apologized for keeping him from doing certain activities and firmly remind me that he was a "lifer" and hadn't married me to hike but married me to love and serve, however that looked. I knew he was on his knees sourcing his strength from God to be able to love me through this season.

Once Tubie invaded my abdominal space, I was unable to swim. The pool is my happy place during the summer in Arizona. We had been going to our friend's pool nearby. I knew I could not submerge my feeding tube in the water, but I could float on top of the water on her giant lobster float!

I loved figuring out that I could still participate in some of the activities that I enjoyed so much. One day, I decided to try getting on the back of our tandem bike. As I was building up my strength and stamina, I found that I could still enjoy biking despite having a feeding tube! We found ourselves doing what we coached our clients to do. We were applying the principle of *get up and live* to our own lives. For me, that meant float time on the pool and short bike rides on the back of the bike.

"Surely," I thought, "If I could pedal on the back of the tandem bike, I could also use my beach cruiser."

Chuck

After working in the Arizona heat for years designing and installing landscaping, heat doesn't really bother me. But my dear wife absolutely despises the heat. One day we realized we could continue our nonprofit work by working from anywhere, especially if it meant getting out of the Arizona heat. Since I am always ready to get to the ocean, we planned a trip to San Diego.

With Covid pushing restaurant seating from inside to out on the streets, we found that we really enjoyed sitting outside surrounded by plants and festive lights, making everything more scenic than sitting in a restaurant. We biked all over the Little Italy area, went to the beach on Coronado Island, met so many amazing people, and just had a blast. Every time we biked past a street musician, I would stop the bike and ask Hannah to dance. My life was like a dream and I kept thanking God.

We had one more important thing to do before we left the coast. Hannah had a couple of books written by a guy named Bob Goff. As a New York Times bestseller, Bob speaks all over the world sharing lessons that are important and relatable to everyone. Unbelievably, even though he was so well known, Bob included his phone number in the back of his books and talked about being available. So I called him.

The first time I tried Bob's number, I got his voice mail. The second time, a couple of days later, I heard a very recognizable voice on the other end. "Hello, this is Bob," he said.

"Hey Bob, Chuck Keels here from Phoenix, how are you doing?"

"Pretty good Chuck, What can I do for you?"

"Well, my wife and I are headed over to San Diego in a few weeks and we would love to say hi."

To my surprise, Bob said even though he was super busy, that we should call him when we get there and he would work something out. We were both jumping up and down and Hannah even took my picture while I was chatting with Bob on the phone. It was on the last day of our trip that I called Bob and set up the meeting.

Hannah and I were looking out at the harbor when an SUV pulled up and out came Bob Goff. I was impressed because he was a successful attorney who had started helping needy people in different parts of the world. He teaches others around the globe how to strengthen their faith by trying new things no matter how difficult they seem. Since I was sharing my cancer story all over the place and telling people about the power of God, I had questions for someone who had already been there.

So I asked Bob, "What is your job title?" I asked this since he didn't go to school to be a pastor, but found himself speaking in churches and retreats all over the world.

Bob looked right at me and said, "I'm just a dude."

And I looked right back at Bob and said, "Then I am just a dude, too."

We shared a great conversation and Hannah showed him a picture that was taken a couple of years earlier over in England. That photo was of Bob and Hannah. He could not believe it. He enjoyed learning about our cancer journeys and how we were building a foundation to help others. He encouraged us to *Dream Big!* (which is the name of his latest book), to keep going, and to keep writing. We took Bob's advice and will catch up with him again someday to fill him in on our journey.

For our next adventure, we headed back to northern Arizona to work and play in Flagstaff and Sedona. And we love having my miniature Australian shepherd, Jax, join us. Not only is he loving and ridiculously smart, but he attracts so many people who want to pet him or at least ask what kind of dog he is. He is by far the best icebreaker I have ever seen. The next thing you know, we are sharing our story, giving these dog-lovers Living Hope Cancer Foundation bracelets, hugging, and exchanging numbers. This is a hoot and I love it.

While in Flagstaff, we discovered a lake nearby called Lake Mary and we loved spending time there. After working up an appetite, we found a cute restaurant called Eat n' Run that advertised a healthy delicious menu, and when we pulled in, the first thing we noticed was they had worship music playing. To display your faith like that was right up our alley and we told the young girl taking our order that we loved the music. She said that we should meet the owner who was in the back office, and the next thing we knew, Wes came out and introduced himself. We told Wes and his wife Sarah our cancer journey story and, just like everyone else, they were blown away. Wes said, "This is kind of cool. Our head pastor is sitting out front having lunch right now." A few minutes later, the pastor came in and Wes introduced everyone before we all got in a big huddle and prayed for Hannah. As always, that results in a lot of energy brought about by the Holy Spirit. And when this happens, I like to say that "church just broke out." This can happen anywhere, at any time, and I truly love it. To this day, we have become good friends with Wes and Sarah and have even gone back up to Flagstaff to speak to their church family.

This was all a part of God's plan!

Another amazing part of this trip was getting red dirt on our shoes in Sedona. With its beautiful views and sunsets, it's one of our favorite places. Even though we had to walk at a slow pace due to Hannah losing her breath and feeling winded, we enjoyed taking our sweet time looking at every plant, rock formation, and talking to other hikers. We even ended up walking around the entire bottom of a formation called Bell Rock. I watched Hannah push through, do things people told her she should not be doing, and still have a life even though she was constantly dealing with cancer setbacks, surgery, pain, and treatments. We were getting up and living and teaching others to *get up and live*, regardless of whatever setback they might have in their lives.

CHAPTER FIFTEEN

Get Up And Live

Hannah

"As long as you are alive, be fully alive" is a phrase that I've heard Chuck say often. It's something that God told him early on in his cancer journey and one that has stuck with me when I've been faced with changes and challenges. When I hear that phrase, I think of the time when I recently felt the most alive—on a camping trip with Chuck.

My first camping trip as an adult was a few years ago with my friend, Brigette, in Oregon. Rather than sleep inside the RV on a couch, I chose to sleep outside in a tent, even though it was freezing at night, around 48 degrees Fahrenheit. It was so cold. I remember sleeping in jeans and a hat, bundled in a blanket and thick sleeping bag. But the air was clean and smelled of fresh pine and campfires.

I had heard Chuck talk about camping several times, but I wasn't really excited about the thought of no bathrooms or a place to wash my hands. And because I am legally blind without my contacts, I'm not thrilled at the thought of having no faucet nearby. But after all of the craziness of surgeries and the drama of the previous few months, I had a sudden craving to feel *fully* alive. My feeding tube had been removed in late July and my newfound freedom had me back in the pool. I was free of my neck brace except for car rides, and it felt like I had a new lease on life. The minute I mentioned that I would like to try camping, Chuck had us in Walmart buying a tent, poop shovel, and camp chairs.

With our gear packed, we set off north to Flagstaff to enjoy the cooler temperatures and be off the grid. We slept under the stars, listened to the wind whistle through the tall pines, and gripped our hot coffee cups in the chilly mornings around the fire. I felt alive for three days until I decided I needed a hot shower and the luxury of running water again.

I was still getting chemo once every week for three weeks with 14 days off in between cycles and we squeezed in short trip after short trip that summer to escape the heat and be able to adventure outdoors. One of the activities we both had enjoyed over the years prior to meeting each other was kayaking. We had talked about how we loved riding our tandem bike together, so why not get a double kayak? Chuck found a used one on Facebook Marketplace and negotiated the life jackets and brand new paddles into the deal.

Our double kayak went on its "Maiden Voyage" in Lake Havasu when our friend Dara invited us to use her beautiful river house. We packed up our dog, Jax, and strapped the kayak to the roof of our car, and headed off on our next adventure. It felt like we were constantly being invited to use people's homes that summer. We were living in God's economy and He was moving people to share what they had with us.

Every day we woke up and said "Yes," to God. Our prayer each morning began with, "Show us where you want us to go and who you want us to meet." It changed our lives together. We recognized that we were on a mission for Him. He brought people to us wherever we were, whether in a coffee shop or ringing our front doorbell. Each person became an opportunity to share our story and point people to Him.

Chuck

As Hannah and I started building our foundation and making it a priority every day to tell our story, I started having friends ask me how we were able to do so. In my old life, I had been a hustler, a sales guy, a mover, and a shaker. I remember walking Jax one morning very upset after a big business deal went south and in the middle of my ranting and complaining I heard a voice tell me that I was already rich. I talked out loud to God reminding Him that I had kids, a house, car payments, etc. But before I could finish, I heard the same thing again.

"You're already rich."

God told me to look at my life, my friends, at how much I enjoyed hiking and walking on the beach.

He said, "There are people in this world with huge bank accounts that are so unhappy they take their own life. So why don't you take money off the table?"

But how was I going to do this? I had chased the dollar my entire life. Little by little, however, I stopped wanting more stuff, worldly things, houses, and bigger trucks. Then for the first time in my life, I started turning down landscaping jobs. Man, did that feel good. I read in the Bible that God would provide, and He does. Our world was changing slowly and, despite all of the challenges we were going through, we were finding a way to have a life.

On one of the trips to Flagstaff's cooler weather, Hannah told me not to plan anything for one of the days. And that's all she would say. We got in the car heading to a surprise destination and my co-pilot gave me turn-by-turn instructions right up to the fairgrounds on the outside of town. She had this big smile on her face and told me we were going on a surprise date! She had me laughing, but still curious. As we drove into this large gated area, I saw signs that said "Zip Line." No way! Hannah had recently been through some very serious health concerns, but now we were going zip lining? I looked at her and asked whether she could really do this, and she told me that she could. And remember, that Extreme Zipline in Flagstaff is no joke.

After we got our gear, instructions, and met our guide, we found ourselves high in the pines. There I stood and watched my wife—the woman who had overcome hurdles and pushed forward in our journey when I don't know if I would have handled things the same way—step off that first platform and soar high above the ground to the next tree stand. I blinked back my happy tears once again, praying that God would send us on many more adventures.

Hannah

I left the Extreme Adventure Park completely exhausted but happy. I could feel that I was pushing up against my physical limits, but it was giving me a really good sense of what I could and could *not* do. And it was showing me that I could push through more than I thought. It helped to have a very motivated partner who was always willing to go on an adventure and simultaneously conscientious about my abilities. I was determined not to stay in bed with the covers pulled up. That was always the easier option: to sit and watch Netflix all day and succumb to the rituals of mind-numbing and checking out. I'd done that before on my own. I imagine that we all can be tempted to go there. But I had a life to live. I didn't want to miss out on meeting new people and trying new things and crossing things off my bucket list. Now I had a best friend to enjoy life with, even if it looked a little different than I had previously imagined, without neck fusions and feeding tubes.

The rest of August was filled with kayaking, visiting yet another friend's mountain home, and an unforgettable trip to a winery. We met friends at a beautiful scenic winery to catch up and enjoy the outdoor views. Even though pandemic precautions were still in place, we could sit mask-free in the wood chairs on the beautiful green sprawling lawns.

As we walked by a small group of people towards the big swing hanging from a high branch, I overheard someone ask, "Is that

Hannah?" At this point, I was unmistakably bald and must have been easy to recognize from our frequent social media posts. Even though we were two hours away from home, someone recognized me. It amused me. And it humbled me. These were people engaged in my story. Praying for me. Concerned for me. And it gave me that added reminder that in my small way of "influencing," I had a profound responsibility to live my life authentically. I didn't want to be *that* person who only posted the highlights and smiles. I also wanted to post about my struggles and how I got through the hard spaces in my life. I cried in Chuck's arms a lot when I had to navigate the physical pain or the disappointment of yet another loss.

One of the hardest losses I experienced that summer was losing my voice. I continued to have ongoing swallowing difficulties, but that didn't explain why my voice was hoarse. I couldn't talk for more than ten minutes without needing to rest my voice for a few hours before I was able to speak again. Singing was out of the question, even though it was one of my favorite things to do in life. I had sung in choirs since I was a little girl and was known for having a good voice in church. I loved to blend notes and harmonize, and it was how I worshipped out loud. Now I found myself in church, covered with a mask, and barely whispering the words to the hymns.

During this time, the nature of my worship completely changed. Instead of belting out the words to make them *sound* nice, I was confined to thinking about each word without speaking it out loud. At first, I cried and cried at the loss of my voice. It was a genuine loss. The grief was real. But then

I began to see the value of worshipping from inside of my being. It took on a different dimension and emotion. It came from deep inside of my spirit. It was a lesson I needed to learn of how to worship in both spirit and truth.

My prayer warriors began to pray for the restoration of my voice. People I had never met, on social media and national and global prayer lists, were praying for me. If God was calling me to share my testimony both on stage and online, surely I would need a working voice to do it. Even if the Ear, Nose and Throat specialist thought that I would never sing again because my vocal cord muscle was paralyzed, I knew that I served a God that could heal me.

CHAPTER SIXTEEN

Cancer Roadmap Project

Chuck

We started Living Hope Cancer Foundation because it was our passion and purpose to take our pains and experiences and share the lessons we learned from them with the hope of helping as many people as we could. The coaching calls and emails came in every day because they, or someone they loved, was diagnosed with cancer, and somehow after a search, they found us. If individuals don't know how to cultivate hope and tap into the positive mindset of a cancer journey, hearing from us can become a big warm blanket. Most of the calls we receive start out with a very worried and scared voice on the other end of the line. We want to know what type of cancer they are talking about, what stage it is, and what their game plan is. We also talk about what state they live in, what they do for work, and a little about family and loved ones around them. In a lot of cases, we are on speakerphone with multiple people listening in. We like that because it's then not just a journey for the individual, but one in which a team is there for support. This is very important because we know what can happen once someone starts treatment. It's very tough on the body physically, and can also mess with you mentally. It's not uncommon to go from fear and freak-out mode to fight mode. But the human mind is so powerful that once you bring a "Get Up and Live" attitude into the equation, things can change on a huge scale.

One day when we were on a conference call with our foundation's board of directors talking about what we had going on, all the time we were spending on the phone and our upcoming plans, they asked us how we were going to be able to keep up with all the activity as things continued growing over the next six months to a year. We answered that we had no idea. Back when I was in the landscaping business and things got really busy, I would just buy another truck and hire more employees. I had no idea what to do next with our cancer foundation, especially since all the time required to talk to and encourage someone during one of the toughest times in their lives is extremely exhausting. One of our board members suggested that we create a video library of coaching videos that anyone could view at any time, watch them as many times as they would like, and even share with others—and all for free. We wanted to make sure that cancer patients and their caregivers would never have to pay a cent for this help. We decided to create a video series consisting of 2-4 minute videos that would walk someone through a cancer journey based on the real-life experience of two Stage 4 cancer thrivers.

As we were on coaching calls over the next few weeks, we paid attention to various topics that came up and then wrote them in a notebook. We ended up with 36 very important topics that we felt would help someone through a cancer journey or through any tough life challenge. We thought about going into a formal studio to produce these coaching videos, but we decided that as we traveled we would take time to make the recordings ourselves. So that means every one of the videos are of Hannah and me. Also because we were talking with cancer patients and caregivers every day, the topics were near and dear to our hearts. Anyone who watches these will see that there are no starts, cuts, or add-ins. We would hit the record button on our cell phone cameras and speak from the heart.

After putting the videos together, our Cancer Road Map Project was born while we took a few trips around Arizona and California. We were excited to be able to share this much-needed, powerful tool with the world. In our own personal experiences, we found that you would get your cancer diagnosis and medical plan just dumped on you—and then start freaking out as you went home. After just hearing the word "cancer," you start trying to process what that means given that you might have kids, grandkids, a husband, or a wife. Most people feel that they aren't ready to deal with that. And the truth of the matter is, nobody is. The problem that Hannah and I determined was the lack of ongoing support. Sure some nonprofits provide meals, or help with cleaning your house, or provide wigs and bras, but getting mindset coaching meant paying big bucks to hire a professional psychiatrist or mental behavior coach. Even with a loving support system around them, people were still worrying, stressing out, and eventually becoming depressed.

Hannah

As we created these videos, I was very much bald and very much in the middle of chemotherapy. I had fatigue on "day 3" after chemo, so I would give myself the entire day off just to lay around, watch TV, and rest. I picked which day of the week I would receive treatment and planned my Off Day. I found that if I had a day of rest, I was so productive the remainder of the week. This was how we were able to create the Cancer Roadmap Project straight out of our experience, quite literally. It's how we designed our clothing line and made an online store: Living Hope Store. I was often amazed at how much we got accomplished but recognized that God had divinely paired two "doers" together for a reason. We loved projects and we asked God's blessing over every bit of them. We both had gotten in the daily habit of seeking Him first and we brought that into our marriage relationship and into our work. We were sourcing our strength from God. We weren't just living this out in front of each other, or the boys still living at home with us, but in front of thousands of friends following us on social media. There were moments where I felt useless as I was struggling through yet another surgery or treatment until I came to realize that was a big fat lie from the enemy. My faith and my daily supernatural strength making sure I "got up and lived" was an example for many people that were watching. It inspired them to not give up, but to keep living. It also motivated them to look to Jesus for their strength. I was living proof that it was possible to go through the valleys of life, the really dark hard places, and have complete peace and joy. I had learned to surrender all of my fears and let God carry them. I could cry it all out to Jesus. Sometimes it became an hourly and daily activity, but the end result was always the same. Complete peace. And with that peace, I could smile at my unknown future. It didn't matter anymore *when* I was going to die, or from what. God had a perfect plan for my life (and for everyone) and I wanted to live my best life for Him.

Some days that would look like a lot of resting. Some days it was busy building a website to help serve people with cancer. Whatever each day looked like, I could see that I could live it for Him and not just for myself. It changed everything. And the fact that I had a life partner with the same conviction was a gift. We were on a mission together, could encourage each other when we needed it, and hold each other's hands as we helped serve others.

As the weeks went by after launching the Cancer Roadmap Project—both on our website and on YouTube—we began receiving emails and messages on social media from people who were watching the videos. People from as far away as India, Brazil, Pakistan, and Spain were sending us messages about how the videos were helping them and their family members affected by cancer. Before this, we hadn't even considered having an impact beyond the United States since we were a domestic nonprofit. But here was proof that our videos were beginning to impact people internationally. Cancer knows no boundaries, whether race, religion, ethnicity, or financial status. It has no borders. So we found it amazing that we were able to help people all over the world. God was blessing our small effort beyond what we had planned or even imagined, which gave us a new drive to continue sharing the lessons we had learned through both of our cancer journeys. It's pretty uncommon to find two Stage 4 cancer thrivers married to each other and committed to coaching others through their journeys with cancer.

We recognized this unique calling that God had placed on our lives and wanted to keep saying "Yes" to Him every day, however that looked.

CHAPTER SEVENTEEN

Singing, Biking, & Moving

Hannah

It had been a long 11 months since I had seen my parents. Covid had canceled their plans to visit in February. They weren't comfortable flying on an airplane so they made plans to rent a mid-sized RV and travel across the country from North Carolina to Arizona. It was an adventure they'll never forget as they "shook" their way across the country for eight days, staying at campgrounds, cooking their own meals, and viewing the passing countryside mile after long mile.

When they arrived, at last, it was a tearful reunion. I had never seen my mother with her hair all gray before, and she had never seen me bald. Chuck and I spent ten days getting spoiled by her cooking, sitting under the stars on the driveway together in the evenings, and having great conversations. This was the second time Chuck had met them and he had a lot of life to catch up on. He took my dad on walks with our dogs, food store runs, and his first kayak ride. They were building a father-son relationship.

One night, Chuck was playing worship music quietly while we were enjoying dinner outside. My favorite song began to play. I began to sing along with a clear strong voice, something I had been unable to do for months! We just began to cry. God was healing my voice and my parents got to be a witness to it. It was another beautiful blessing realizing that we serve a God who can restore things that had been lost.

Chuck

Before God put Hannah in my life, I was a 55-year-old who had started to think I was going to grow old alone. I was not happy about this because I wanted to have someone in my life who I can make laugh and make memories with. After Hannah and I got together, something I did not think about is that I didn't just marry her; I married a whole new family. The time we spent with her parents, Papa and Mama, was like a breath of fresh air. We could sit and talk for hours like we had known each other for years. And I thought it was great they came to see us via a cross-country adventure in a rented RV. That sounded like something I would love to do.

Their visit was right on time because their beautiful daughter had been through so much and I knew that Hannah needed her parents here and they needed to help take care of their daughter.

During their visit, Hannah and I still had a ton of things going on like coaching, working on the foundation, and preparing for our next fundraiser—a biking fundraiser. Hannah's breathing was not good due to a cancerous node pushing on her carotid artery and airway, so the discussion came up about an electric bike (or ebike) because they give the rider some extra assistance. We knew this was going to be the only way we were going to get Hannah on a bike, so I started doing my homework. The well-known brand names had ebikes but the prices were way out of our price range. I came across a bike that had fat tires which I loved. You can fold them up for storage or while traveling and they were less than $1000. I called Lectric XP ebike company to ask questions and I was thrilled that they were based right here in Phoenix. I told them our cancer story and how it was jeopardizing Hannah's breathing, which had led us to research ebikes. When I finished the explanation, a very friendly voice on the other end of the phone asked us if we could come in to see their facilities. We were happy to do so; it sounded like fun to us. We set up an appointment and a couple of days later walked into the front door of Lectric XP. They were giving customers test rides and teaching them how to use the new electric-assist bikes, which was really exciting. We met the owners and the staff. They showed us all around the facilities and our tour ended in the warehouse. Our guide told us an interesting story. She said that normally they only made black bikes and white bikes, but they had special-ordered two beautiful soft pink bikes. One of those bikes was for the owner's wife and they hadn't yet decided what to do with the other one. Then she told us that after hearing our story, they knew they wanted to give that bike to Hannah. We were surprised and completely overwhelmed.

Hannah and I stood there with tears in our eyes. Hannah's dad had plans to buy her one so he ended up buying me a bike so I could keep up with Hannah. The ebikes have entirely added a whole new window of adventure into our lives and allowed us to *"get up and live."*

Hannah

Once my parents left to return home, we realized it was time to think about finding a new place to live. Our landlady had been talking about flipping the house we were renting and, legally, she was only required to give us 30 days' notice. Since I was in active treatment, we decided we wanted to be in charge of the timing for a move.

Our friend Linda mentioned that her sister had just bought an investment property in South Scottsdale and was looking for renters. She gave us the address and we decided to ride our new electric bikes to check it out. I immediately *knew* this was our next home as soon we walked in. It was a perfect size and had a wonderfully bright room we could use as our home office. The bonus was we would be moving into a neighborhood with our cousin Heather across the street, our friends Mark and Linda three doors away, and our family pastor just around the corner. We already had a built-in community, and there was a giant pool 50 yards from our house. We could see waterways full of ducks and turtles right outside our living room window. We gave our landlady our 30-day notice and began the process of sorting through every closet and bin.

Chuck

We love to live the lifestyle we call *Get up and live* and it became our purpose to encourage others to do the same. *Get up and live* simply means; don't waste time even if you are facing a big setback. We've discovered that *Get up and live* is the answer to a lot of problems. For one thing, you engage your mind when you start thinking about doing something active like walking your dog, going for a bike ride, leaving for a family vacation, or just getting down on the living room floor to stretch. Then the physical action follows.

We love *Get up and live* so much that when the topic came up of getting matching tattoos to exemplify how we were growing closer and experiencing life together, the obvious design would be *Get up and live*. We both laughed when the idea came up and immediately agreed to move forward. We set up an appointment to get the ink, but we didn't know much about the shop we chose. We walked in and started chatting with a handsome young tattoo artist and we couldn't believe what he told us. He said they considered themselves to be a faith-based shop and they even hosted open Bible study there every Friday night. Can you believe that? But you can't make up stuff like this. The matching lifetime tattoos were completed, and Hannah and Chuck Keels now have a huge reminder that when things get heavy, we can glance down at our forearms for a reminder to suck it up and *Get up and live*!

We got those tattoos around the same time we signed the lease on that sweet little condo that sits on a man-made waterway. We were excited about starting a new chapter, but we weren't sure how the move was going to take place since Hannah was dealing with a lot: recovering from surgery, chemo treatment, daily fatigue, and pain.

So we started by sorting through closets. Since she wasn't allowed to lift anything, Hannah would point and I would do the heavy work. I put boxes of stuff on our table, and she sorted through them. We got the keys two weeks before we could actually move into our new place and our amazing landlord said we could bring things over and leave them in the house. So this added a new element to our preparation. Hannah could now sort things into one area that needed to be tossed out, set up another area for thrift store donations, and then the third area for things we could not live without that needed to go to our new home. I borrowed a trailer from my cousin and every day we would make a trip to the new place. I would unload everything, lock up, and head back home. My biggest concern was that Hannah normally started feeling fatigued mid-afternoon --- which meant she was done for the day and needed to rest through the evening. But all of the sorting work was keeping her on her feet until dinner time. I kept asking her to stop and rest, but she always told me it was her stuff and nobody else would know what to do with it.

Hannah

And I was right about needing to sort everything myself. (I often am. We'd been married almost an entire year by this point.) Just as I certainly would not have been comfortable throwing away Chuck's things if they had value to him, I knew I had to sort my own things. I was not only canvassing through my own personal items but also having to decide whether to keep or discard my boys' things. By this time, three of my boys were living on their own, sharing an apartment together. My youngest, Lucas, was almost 18 years old and was planning to move out a week before our official moving day. Not only was I going through the emotions of "losing" a son, (well, at least the joy of daily interactions with my baby) I also had to navigate what to keep and what to get rid of. We were moving to a condo that did not have a lot of storage for extra things. I sorted through all of my old photo albums and made each of the boys a bin of their own pictures. I no longer was going to store their "stuff" if they had their own apartments.

I was beginning to feel the full weight of becoming an "empty nester." I cried a lot and Chuck just held me. My biggest fear just a year earlier had been what to do once my boys decided to move out and I would be left all alone.

God had provided the exact right someone to fill that void. At just the right time.

CHAPTER EIGHTEEN

Who Walks Around With A Broken Back?

Chuck

All of our stuff that made the move was now at the new place piled up all over the house. Normally, I would put the beds together and fill the drawers with all of our stuff and make this new place home, but we ran into a problem. The remodeling that was supposed to have been done before we moved in wasn't even close to being completed. And the really big problem, other than having to share our new place with four or five construction dudes who continually came in and out with dusty boots, was that the bathrooms were completely ripped apart. Although there are a lot of things you can work around, you're going to need a bathroom sooner than later. Thank God for beautiful friends like Linda and Mark who we knew from church and lived across the alley. They graciously spoke up and said they had an extra bedroom and bathroom and it was all ours until our new place was ready. Not only did we have a big soft bed, but we also had the love and conversation from Linda and Mark. God knew we needed that.

Even though we weren't staying at our new place, we started getting things ready. On day one, we tackled setting up most of the kitchen cabinets and drawers. With the construction going on all day, every night once the crew left I would get out the vacuum to clean all the floors and then mop them. I knew it would not eliminate all of the dust, but with Hannah's breathing being jeopardized from the cancer and treatment, I was doing my best to clear the air.

It was the end of the day and we were beyond exhausted. We headed over to Linda and Mark's for a hot shower and a good night's sleep. We climbed in bed, I gave Hannah a good night kiss and hit the pillow. I'm one of those guys that are knocked out as soon as I lay down and tonight I think I fell asleep as I was laying down because I was that tired.

At about 1:30 in the morning, Hannah woke me up and said, "I'm in pain and I can't sit up. Can you help me to the bathroom?"

I pulled back the covers and literally put my arms under her armpits and lifted her up. This forklift escort went all the way to the bathroom as she kept saying, "What is wrong with me?" I started to take her back to bed when Hannah asked me to put her on the living room couch which was right outside the bedroom. I grabbed some pillows and blankets, got her comfortable, and went back to bed.

Who Walks Around With A Broken Back?

I was scared. What was causing the pain? I dozed off a couple of times but was listening for Hannah. Finally, at 4:30 I went back out to check on her and she said, "I can't move." Immediately I called 9-1-1 and the operator said the first responders were on their way.

Now remember, we are at Linda and Mark's place and a fire truck pulls up out front. I went out to meet them to tell them what was going on with Hannah and to give them directions on how to get inside. Several of the firefighters were talking to Hannah and taking vital signs and several more were out front getting a stretcher ready. One of the guys from out front came in and told me that we had a small problem. Due to the brick archways leading into the house, the stretcher wouldn't fit inside. One of the other guys then jumped up without hesitation, went out, and came back in with a big bag with handles on it that would work as a more flexible stretcher. But to get the bag under her, they needed to roll Hannah forward and then back onto it. When the rolling started, I heard Hannah holler out in agonizing pain.

Chills went up my spine and as I watched the team lift Hannah up. My mind went straight back to the day I had suffered a spinal collapse from my cancer spreading and ended up on the floor with eight first responders around me. The mind can put you in a tough place at times, and all I could do was stand there, watch history repeat itself, and cry. My wife was being taken to a hospital in exactly the same way I had been loaded up, just five years earlier.

We had not even been married a year and in the cold Arizona morning, I watched the door shut on the ambulance as it drove off with Hannah for the second time.

Hannah

I knew there was something wrong with my lower back. The pain was excruciating. I was experiencing sharp jabbing pain and I couldn't get comfortable in any position. The ambulance ride to the hospital seemed to last an eternity, while in reality, it was only six minutes away from our house. Every turn and bump was agonizing. The first responders couldn't give me any pain medication until they were able to properly diagnose me. It was December 16, a week before Christmas. This was not my idea of a cozy holiday experience. This was miserable.

What was happening?

All I could do was pray.

At last, they wheeled me into the Emergency Room and slid me onto a slightly bigger stretcher. Again, due to COVID restrictions, I had to do it all alone: answer all their questions, experience the waiting, and make the decisions required. Very quickly, I was whisked over to the imaging room to have a CT scan done.

The ER doctor came in and sat down. "You have a fractured sacrum," she said. "It's related to cancer in the area. The fracture is running up and down the right side of your pelvis. I'm going to talk to a specialist and see what they recommend."

"Not again!" I moaned to myself. I couldn't believe that the cancer had spread to the lower spine while I was on chemotherapy and immunotherapy 3 days a month.

"We are going to admit you to the floor," said the doctor after speaking to the spine specialist. "We need to get your pain under control," she said.

I had to call Chuck and break the news to him. Now he wasn't the only one walking around with a broken back.

I was admitted to my room and spent the rest of the day extremely uncomfortable. Nothing was helping my pain. We tried narcotics and they didn't touch it. I was nauseous and miserable, curled up in a fetal position. Doctor after doctor came in to assess me, including an oncologist and a spinal specialist. I could barely have a conversation with them. When I could manage to text, I asked Chuck to put out a prayer request for me on Facebook. Finally, I told the nurse to stop giving me narcotics and just to give me a dose of anti-inflammatory medication. Exhausted, I fell asleep and woke up two hours later without the excruciating pain I had been experiencing. It was manageable and I could sit up in bed for the first time. The doctors did a double-take the next morning when I was sitting up in bed and conversing as if I was a completely different patient.

I called Chuck and said, "Pick me up Babe, I'm ready to come home."

He was shocked. Maybe he should know better by now! I had thousands of people praying for me and I had no intention of staying in the hospital for any longer than necessary. As long as I could keep managing my pain, my only restriction was to avoid lifting. The fracture was not operable. It just needed time to heal.

When I got home, I could see that Chuck had been busy. Typically, I set up my Christmas tree the day after Thanksgiving. I absolutely love the holidays and this year had felt so strange because of our move. I came home to a lit Christmas tree awaiting my decorations! Several friends had offered to help Chuck while I was in the hospital. They set up the tree, helped him move around the furniture, and set up our living room and bedroom. It was such a pleasant surprise to come home to a more organized space. All of a sudden, our construction zone became home. We knew that we had a few more weeks with our crew wandering in and out, but we were taking back our house for the holidays. A few days later, I was sitting on the couch giving Chuck directions as to where to hang each ornament. We made the best of our situation. Every day was a new opportunity to live and breathe. Each day was a gift from God. The more hard stuff we were experiencing, the more of a reality that became.

We had a lovely low-key Christmas with just the two of us, our first time not spending it with the boys. On January 1st, I surprised Chuck by walking into the room with my wedding dress on. We were going to spend the entire day celebrating a full year of marriage. It had been a crazy year full of fun and not-so-fun things. But we wouldn't change any of it for all of the lessons that we had learned. We had learned to love each other deeper, to be more patient with each other, and where to place our hope. When we had made our vows "for better or for worse, in sickness and in health," we hadn't the foggiest clue that our year would be full of cancer progression, fractured spines (of both the top and bottom), a feeding tube for almost 2 months, and more hospital visits than we could count that would keep us apart. COVID made the time apart more lonely, but it had made our bond even tighter.

We still had managed to travel, explore, start a nonprofit, run fundraisers, and find new ways to *get up and live* no matter what.

2020 had turned out to be a year full of blessings despite the hurdles.

Chuck

Everyone tries to understand what it's like to face these types of challenges and adversities. Going through a journey with cancer, and now coaching cancer patients daily, I know way more about the human body and how both cancer and its treatments affect it. Our anniversary was a huge test of my faith. Before Hannah's most recent physical challenges, I had been thinking of plans to surprise my beautiful wife for our first anniversary. Now, not only were the plans shut down, but they were the furthest thing from my mind as I worried about her health. When she walked into the room in that wedding dress on January 1st, our one-year anniversary, time stood still. My heart melted all over again, just like the year before when we made a promise to each other in front of God and all of our friends.

CHAPTER NINETEEN

The Inspiration Tour

Hannah

The year 2021 began within a renewed commitment to each other to love one another regardless of what we would face. We had already proven that was possible the previous year because we both were sourcing our strength from God. We were both learning to wear our faith like it was our skin. We made a constant effort to be transparent and share our journey with our friends and family. They got to see all the good and the bad. I've never had so many cheerleaders in my life, and it reiterated the importance of what we were doing as cancer coaches: cheering our clients on in life.

We continued doing whatever activities we could. I knew I couldn't paddle a kayak but I *could* sit in one. We packed up our car and drove the four miles to our closest body of water,

Tempe Town Lake. Chuck had to do all of the heavy lifting and dragged our double kayak to the water's edge and carefully helped situate me on a cushion. I wedged the life jacket around me to stabilize my spine as we kayaked around the lake. We had a beautiful hour on the water enjoying our music and watching the clouds and birds. It wasn't a huge endeavor, but I was able to get out of the house and experience nature. Two weeks later, I was on my electric bike, cruising the bike paths near our house. I couldn't bend over to pick up a tissue I had dropped, but I could go biking. In the past, I probably would have limited myself because of my restrictions, but now I felt like I needed to *get up and live!*

My constant question was, "What *can* I do?" It changed everything for me. And I wasn't the only one asking that question.

Chuck

An ongoing discussion that we had with each other and our clients was focused on how we don't really know our limits until we try things. *Get up and live*, right? Hannah was gradually starting to feel a little better and I was dying to do something for her to celebrate our first year of marriage, even though our anniversary had already passed.

I asked Hannah, "Can you ride in the car for two hours?"

She replied, "I think so."

"Then would you like to go to Sedona?"

The Inspiration Tour

We both love the beauty of the Red Rocks and the peace and tranquility there. Hannah did not jump at the offer like she normally would.

She said, "I can't hike so what are we going to do?"

"We can relax and enjoy each other's company!" I replied.

"Deal!"

So that sounded like there wasn't anything exciting planned, right? Wrong!! I was hard at work on the phone that week. What could we do there that wouldn't involve hiking? I drove Hannah around the town and told her about a cute restaurant on top of a butte. When we got up there, she commented that it also looked like an airport—and I told her that it was. So instead of driving up to the restaurant, I drove to an airport hangar. Hannah saw a sign that said *Sedona Air Tours* and asked me if we were going up in a helicopter. Smiling from ear to ear, I told her that we were. I had already explained to the tour company what our situation was and about the tough year that Hannah had had. For the first time in her life, Hannah climbed into the seat of a Rolls Royce helicopter and sat down next to the pilot. Now you would think that cruising over Sedona would be enough, but God thought He would add a special touch of His own. As we lifted off, we saw a Sedona sight that only a few get to see each year: the entire area was lightly dusted with snow and was absolutely breathtaking. The smile on Hannah's face was even more beautiful than that snow on Sedona's red rock.

There is no way that anyone could be on the journey God put us on and not grow and change. One night over dinner I told Hannah that I had been baptized as a baby, but I had changed so much that I was feeling called to get baptized as an adult. Two weeks later, we got up on a Sunday morning and Hannah was not feeling well. We normally go to church at 9 a.m. and I told Hannah to rest and that it would be okay if we missed church. About two hours later, she said she was actually feeling a lot better and still wanted to go to church. So I suggested we go somewhere we don't normally go and Hannah wanted to try Hillsong in downtown Phoenix. I was thinking that it would be super cool because we often watched Pastor Terry Crist at Hillsong church on TV.

When we arrived at church, we were greeted by a young group of energetic Hillsong people and I just *had* to share my miraculous story of healing from stage 4 cancer. The more I got into the story, the more their energy lifted and they were cheering like we were at a Phoenix Suns game. At the end, one of the girls looked at me and asked whether I'd been baptized. I said I was baptized as a baby but I didn't remember it. Unbelievably, she told me that they were baptizing at church that day! Emotion came over me and God said, "It's time." I took a couple of steps over to a pew, sat down, and started crying. I knew it was time.

As the church service started, the young man sharing the announcements asked if there were any first-timers in attendance. With about 20 others throughout the crowd, I raised my hand. The young man on the stage asked me my name.

I answered in a surprised voice, "Chuck."

Everyone in the church of over 200 then said, "Welcome, Chuck!"

I was like, what just happened? The baptism was outside in the courtyard and to my surprise, there were over sixty people lined up to take the dip and declare their faith. Their families and friends were cheering them on and it was beautiful. I was the last one in line and, when I stepped into the pool, people started hollering, "Way to go, Chuck!!!" Hannah was holding my hand and I knew that with the events that had changed my life in the past few years, that I wanted to be as close as possible to Jesus.

As I was pulled up from the water, I felt His unconditional love wash over me.

That feeling even carried over into the next morning as we headed to a breakfast place in downtown Scottsdale for a meeting. On the way there, I looked at Hannah and asked her if she wanted to hear something amazing. I then told her how, for some reason, everything around me looked brighter.

Hannah

As the days flew by, we knew that it was time to make a trip to see both sets of parents. As we began to plan for our trip to Ohio and North Carolina, we decided to add in a stop in Pennsylvania where I had spent nearly a decade of my life. It became apparent that we would have several opportunities to speak on our trip.

The more we talked about it, the more speaking events began to form in each leg of our journey. We jokingly referred to our trip as "The Inspiration Tour. " A family member donated airline miles to us and we were able to fund the travel of our entire trip. A friend suggested we have shirts made for one of the events. Soon local businesses were donating to have their logos placed on the back of the shirts. We ordered "Get up and live" masks to wear on the airplane and sell at the events. We packed our suitcases full of books, mugs, masks, and gear that we sold on our website store. It had become official. We were now actually on "The Inspiration Tour."

We left balmy Phoenix in mid-February and landed in Columbus, Ohio, to slushy snow. The only rental car available by the time we arrived was a 2-seater Mustang. Chuck squeezed all of our luggage into the car and we just had to laugh as we drove through the snow. This was our kind of adventure! We took a lot of COVID precautions so we could stop by and see his mom and dad. Then we headed two hours north to the little town of Fostoria that Chuck had been born and raised in. I finally got to meet many of the people he had spoken about, and many of whom had friended me on Facebook. Our event that Friday evening had 75-80 people in attendance. We were amazed that during a pandemic, so many people were willing to gather.

They were all looking for some hope and our inspirational stories were just the ticket.

We met in a large hall with chairs spaced apart with plenty of hand sanitizer. For some, it was the first time they had gone out in public in a year, and it meant the world to us that they were willing to do so to hear our story. We spoke for 45 minutes, signed books, and sold merchandise and shirts.

Chuck

One lady in the crowd stopped us in the middle of our talk and, with emotion in her voice said, "This story is not just for cancer people. Everyone in the world needs to hear this." We knew we were touching hearts and changing lives by sharing this incredible journey God put us on. And it wasn't just at the speaking events. We shared our story in the airports, restaurants, and hotels, and people were huddling up to pray over Hannah. We even had a TV news crew show up at one of the events and put us on the Ohio news. There were cancer patients showing up who found out about us on social media. You can't make this up. God was rolling it out.

The 2021 Inspiration Tour gained momentum and took us from Ohio to Pennsylvania and then on to North Carolina. We had people come up after the events and tell us they didn't realize how powerful our message was going to be. They then promised to pack the venues the next time we came through. For the rest of our trip, we spent some stops with friends and families and then spent other nights in hotels.

Midway through the tour, Hannah said her back was starting to bother her. We thought for sure it was due to all of the different mattresses.

Hannah

As powerful as it was to tell our story together on stage, it was often in the "in-between" moments that we had the most Spirit-led moments. As we continued to ask God to lead us in every moment of each day, He was teaching me to surrender even in the uncomfortable moments. I've shared earlier about my personal disdain for wheelchairs. I didn't like what they represented to me—the loss of my independence. As we maneuvered our way cross country between states, with a series of one-way flights, my back was hurting more and more. I knew that riding in a wheelchair at the airport would help the pain.

As I requested wheelchair assistance at the gate in Ohio, I was directed to sit and wait in a certain set of blue chairs. A lady had her bags in the adjoining chair and apologized for taking up the extra space, which opened up our conversation to share our story. This led to her and her husband praying over us, asking God to bless our ministry and to heal me. At the next airport where I needed wheelchair assistance, our attendant was a converted Pakistani Muslim. He also asked to pray for healing over me. He prayed out loud with great emotion in Urdu, his native tongue.

In these moments of my own personal discomfort, God was showing me He was with me and surrounding me with His people. I wasn't alone and He knew my exact situation.

CHAPTER TWENTY

Fractured Dreams

Hannah

Arriving home from our *Inspiration Tour* in early March, I knew that I had to get some answers about why my back was hurting so badly. This felt oddly familiar: coming home from a trip and needing to figure out what was wrong with me. My first call was to schedule an X-ray of my pelvis. I knew that my sacral fracture would take some time to heal, but this was pain in a different place on my hip. This was definitely something new. The X-ray did not reveal anything new, but yet the pain persisted. I was living on ibuprofen and my heating pad to get through my days. I knew that I needed to persevere. I wasn't due for a CT scan again for a while so my insurance would not cover one. I felt like I was at a standstill.

Chuck

Hannah had been on a month's break from chemotherapy treatment. We were happy about it because of the toll it takes on the human body. During this time, her hair started to get thicker and stronger and so she let it grow. Since Hannah had long, dark hair when I met her and often wore it in different styles, I was all for her letting it grow back in. But as soon as she started back on chemo, she started finding big clumps of hair in the shower. Our wishful thinking was over. It was time to shave it again.

I got out a chair, a cape, and the hair clippers. I also set up my phone on a tripod so we could share what it's like to go through this emotional ritual, to help others going through it know they are not alone. Hannah put on the cape, and I turned on the clippers, slowly buzzing off her pretty hair. I'm a much bigger baby than Hannah. She always says it's because she is a nurse and I guess nurses are tough. I cried through the haircut and brushed her off. As she stood up, I handed her the clippers so she could shave mine. She got a little emotional and told me I didn't have to do it. But I looked at her and told her we are in this together, no matter what.

So, yes, it was something I needed to do without giving it another thought. In just moments, we were both back to being "skinheads." We cried and hugged. We wanted to be transparent about what this was like for those watching the video. To our surprise, over 20,000 people watched our video and the responses were amazing. That is why we share our journey. It's like a big social media hug.

Now we were ready for the next portion of the 2021 Inspiration Tour in Florida. We were so excited about this speaking tour because we were not only going to get to catch up with close friends Conor and Liz in Celebration, and Tony and Paulette and Cindy and Pete in the Tampa area, but we had multiple speaking events planned. Our flights were booked and a schedule was set.

Hannah

The day before we were planning to fly out of Phoenix to Orlando, Florida, I woke up in agony. I couldn't walk.

Here we go again, I thought.

Chuck called 911 and this time the first responders came to *our* back door, exactly three months after our last call, when we had been staying with friends. Once again, I was loaded onto a stretcher and strapped on for the short ride to the hospital.

Chuck

For the third time for this newly married couple, I watched my wife be taken away in an ambulance.

Hannah

Similar to the previous visit, I had several scans done and the doctors determined that I had a compression fracture of the L4 vertebrae in the lower part of my spine.

Again I wondered, Who walks around with a broken back?

This was now my third experience with a spinal fracture! This felt unreal. I had to call Chuck with the crazy news that I was diagnosed with yet another fracture and was being admitted to the hospital to help manage the pain. Pain management doctors, oncologists, radiation oncologists, the hospitalist, and physical therapists all took turns traipsing through my room to assess me and discuss my options. We decided on some pain medication to get me relatively comfortable. And then I had a walker fitted to my height. It was my first experience having a bedside commode because I could not walk. I had to painfully scoot myself to the foot of the bed and pivot my body in order to use it. Everything hurt.

Thankfully, Chuck was finally allowed to visit since COVID restrictions were loosening. He surprised me by bringing along Jax in his Service Dog collar. I was so happy to see both of them and their visits became the highlight of my days. After two days, the radiation oncologist recommended a radiation treatment of the sacrum and L4 areas to slow the progression of the cancer. This required that I be transferred to another local hospital that had access to radiation equipment. It was the same place I had been to the summer before to receive radiation on my chest node. Once again, I was strapped into an ambulance and transported to another hospital. This was beginning to feel repetitive. I just wanted to be home in my own bed with my own food. Chuck even brought his shaving kit to the hospital and shaved my head for me.

Finally, after three more days in the hospital, I got the okay to go home. I couldn't sit. I couldn't stand. I couldn't walk. But I was home. I spent the next ten days in bed. I had to use a bedside commode. I lost all of my independence. Chuck had to do every single thing for me, from bringing me a cup of tea or a meal, to bringing me my toothbrush and a glass to spit in. I was taking pain medications around the clock, every 2-4 hours on a specific schedule to try to manage the back pain.

I felt so alone even though I had several visitors. I couldn't go outside. I could only lie down in bed. It was a time of deep pondering. I had a lot of questions for God. They weren't terribly new questions. But I asked them all the same. I knew it was okay and He could handle them. He kept reminding me through songs, through the words I read in the Bible, and through different people, that He was also with me in this new trial. He sat with me in my pain and agony. This was the place where I was learning to surrender my will at an even deeper level. I couldn't figure out how He could possibly get glory from my story while I was stuck in bed and unable to share it with others. But then I began to see a few glimpses. Through comments on social media posts from those following my story, and in messages from people I didn't even know, I began to understand how my faith in my suffering was inspiring so many.

On April 1st, less than a month after arriving home from the first leg of our Inspiration Tour, I once again had to call 911 at the advice of my pain doctor and oncologist. The pain wasn't manageable with the narcotics I had been taking and there was no end in sight of being confined to my bed. Unlike the last time when the first responders came, I could no longer hobble to my bedroom door and climb onto the stretcher. And since the entrance to our bedroom was too narrow for a stretcher to be wheeled in, once again I had to be carried from my bed to the stretcher with a big bag. Again I was groaning and moaning. I still had two fractures in my spine that weren't healed.

Chuck

This latest episode of back pain was very upsetting to me. Hannah had been released from the hospital after a big dose of radiation, yet nothing had changed. Even the 20-minute car ride had been agonizing for her even with tons of pillows and blankets to cushion her. Those few days at home had been a huge test of faith for both of us.

Jesus, wake up! The storm is going to sink the boat! Don't you care? What did Jesus say then and what was he saying to us? You need to keep the faith, because those are the times you grow, learn lessons and gain wisdom.

So for the fourth time in a little less than a year, an ambulance pulled up and first responders did their amazing and tough job of carrying Hannah to a stretcher and rolling her out of the house to be transported to the nearest hospital. Once she was in the ER and they did multiple scans and checks of her vital signs, it didn't take long to learn the cancer that had spread in her sacrum was causing all kinds of havoc. Her spine was fractured and breaking down in several places. Then came the news that they were going to transfer Hannah to another hospital that specialized in spinal surgery. They began preparing for emergency surgery the next day.

Hannah

"This is what bone normally looks like," explained the resident as he pointed to a scan image on his phone. "Bone, disc, bone, disc," he continued on, pointing to my L2 and L3 levels, "And bone with a tumor in it," he said as he showed me my L4 level.

Skipping over the disc and intact L5 level, he touched his pen to the screen over a dark area and said, "This is all supposed to be white, it's all supposed to be bone. It's the S1 and S2 area that is now a fused tumor mass. The plan, as of now, is to fuse you from the L3 level down to your hip where we can place some rods and screws. It's not minor surgery," he sighed. And then he started explaining all the possible side effects.

I was in shock. The nurse part of my brain was understanding all of the procedural explanations, but there was another part of me struggling with the implications of this surgery.

Another fusion? I thought, as my mind was trying to stay involved with the conversation. I had already had my neck fused the year before and lost a chunk of my summer to wearing a neck brace and recovering from the surgery. I had to remind myself not to get too far ahead and just take this one minute at a time.

The first task was to call Chuck with the latest news that I was having surgery the following morning to fuse my lower spine.

The next day, Good Friday, I woke up ready for surgery. They told me I would be returned to this same room after surgery, and then they wheeled me away. The night before, I had also met my surgeon and he had grabbed my hand and asked me if he could pray for me. It was another reminder that I was surrounded by God's people.

I can do a 3-hour surgery, I thought to myself bravely as I drifted off to sleep.

Chuck

I spoke to Hannah a little bit the morning of her surgery. She was not in the mood for a conversation, but I got the important stuff: what time they were going to take her down to surgery, how long the preparation would take, what time the procedure would start, and that 2 ½ to 3 hours later she would be finished and back in her room. I did everything I needed to do at home and I planned to get to the hospital around two o'clock that afternoon. I had some things to work on to keep me busy in the waiting room. The surgeon informed me that he would come out when they finished and give me a report. I planned to be in Hannah's hospital room around three o'clock as she came out of surgery so I could be there for her as she woke up.

I watched the clock pass 3:00, and then 4:00. By 4:30, there was still no word. All kinds of things were racing through my mind and the only thing I could do was pray. I finally called a hospital phone number and explained that I was in the waiting room and was looking for information. The next thing I knew, I was on the phone with an operating room nurse. She explained that the procedure was still underway and they would contact me as soon as Hannah's surgery was over.

I started to get emotional. Something was not right—it was taking too long. I called Hannah's mom and dad in North Carolina and I was so emotional I could barely talk. I explained that they had said she would be out of surgery in three hours, but yet it was nearing five hours. Papa told me everything would be okay and he and Mama were praying for Hannah and me. I sat there in the waiting area, nothing short of a snotty mess, and watched the clock go from 5:00 to 6:00, and then 7:00.

Finally, the spinal surgeon walked out. He looked like he had just hiked 100 miles up a mountain. He was taking off the headgear that he wore during surgery, caught his breath, and said to me, "When we opened Hannah up, we were not expecting what we found."

My heart dropped and I could not breathe. He continued, "The cancer has spread much worse than we expected and damaged a lot of bone. The surgery supporting her spine and hip bone area was successful. Although we are not oncologists, we did remove about 50% of the cancer." The doctor said that he was very disappointed that Hannah's oncologist had not been on top of this. I thanked him and he turned and walked out.

The waiting room visiting hours ended at 7:00, but an OR nurse came out and told me they could take me to the post-op area where Hannah was being moved to. I walked in as they were hooking up all of the wires to keep an eye on her vital signs, since being under sedation for over seven hours is very tough on the human body. I held her hand as she was just starting to wake up. Ten or fifteen minutes went by and she slowly looked over at me.

The first thing she said after weeks of being stuck in her bed at home in ridiculous pain was that her back still hurt. Then she said, "Hold my hand." She was in and out of consciousness.

I was a mess.

After an hour went by, the nurse informed me that she was in good hands and suggested I go home and get some rest. I walked to my car wondering, *What had just happened? How did a 3-hour surgery last seven hours?*

I picked up a chicken sandwich and ate it on the way home. I took Jax for a short walk, turned off all of the lights, and dragged my completely exhausted body into the bedroom. I sat down on

the bed and with the light still on, laid back, and passed out with my feet still on the floor. I woke up and saw that it was 4:00 in the morning. I looked over and saw a text on my phone. I was completely surprised. The text was from Hannah and she had sent it at 1:00, three hours before.

It simply said, "What happened to me?"

CHAPTER TWENTY-ONE

Get Up And Walk

Hannah

I woke up disoriented and confused. *Where am I?* I thought to myself since I was supposed to be back in my room and instead, I found myself in the ICU. Apparently, I had received 3 units of blood due to severe blood loss. I was in tremendous pain and couldn't stop vomiting. I was sure it was due to the immense amounts of medications that had been pumped into my body during the extensive surgery. I had scrapes and bruises on my face and arms from extra IVs and having laid on my stomach for the length of the operation. From my own experience as an operating room nurse, I knew that there was a lot of tape involved to keep breathing tubes and IVs in place during a surgery done in the prone position.

I felt like I had been hit by a truck. I guess that's why I had woken up in the ICU and not in my other room.

Thankfully, within a day I was transferred to a regular room and fitted with a back brace. A physical therapist came into the room to explain how to secure the brace around my midsection with Velcro. The next step was to sit on the side of the bed and move to the chair.

The chair? I thought. I hadn't sat up in almost 3 weeks!

Trusting his expertise, I slowly sat up, placed my weight on my feet, and stood up as he supported me. It was unbelievable. Soon, I was walking with a walker and sent home to recuperate, just five days after I was admitted. I had completely missed Easter weekend, but I was so glad to go home to my own bed again. I might have had a 60-staple scar running up my lower back, but I could sit and walk again, even if it was at a granny pace. I could pick a spot in the house to walk to and sit or lie down. It was a small step towards independence that I welcomed wholeheartedly. Even that old borrowed wheelchair was a sight for sore eyes because it became my way back outside to enjoy the birds and trees and sunsets. Chuck returned to full caregiver mode, doing the dishes, laundry, providing meals, and meeting my *every* need.

Chuck

With Hannah in the condition she was in, I couldn't let myself get too far from the house. I shortened my walks with Jax, stopped going to the gym, and ran to the grocery store only when my cousin Heather or our friend Barbara could stay with Hannah.

Full caregiver mode is not just trying to keep the person you love as comfortable as possible, but also sacrificing part of your routine life. I saw it as a huge blessing that I no longer had a full-time landscaping job and was able to be home for Hannah. Being a caregiver is such a hard role both physically and mentally that I had to play a *Chuck mind game*. I told myself I wanted to be the number one caregiver in the world. Period!

Nothing was normal about our lives. Public speaking and sharing our stories had become a big part of our ministry. All of our events were canceled or put on hold. We had a big mountain to climb to get past what Hannah was going through. And as much as I hate to say this, making future plans was tough since we still had her cancer and recovery to deal with. I give Hannah a lot of credit for helping us get through that challenging time. When I was worried about her health and her future, she would step in and say, "This is temporary." This is an important lesson for anyone reading this who is going through difficulty. You can choose to freeze up in fear and stay stuck, or you can tell yourself that it's a temporary state and then move forward.

We had an upcoming plan to speak on a Wednesday evening at Redemption Church in Phoenix as part of a series called "Backstories." This series was to allow members of the community to learn more about their church family. Given our situation, I started to cancel this event several times, but Hannah would not let me.

She said, "I can be tired here on the couch or I can be tired up in front of the church telling everyone our story."

I could not argue with that. So 17 days after a 7-hour spinal surgery and now getting around in a wheelchair, Hannah and I were sitting on stage with Pastor Frank sharing our past and current miracles.

Hannah

Although I saw really great progress after surgery and was thrilled to be back in the pool, I was experiencing a lot of pain in my right hip. Because it was throwing off my balance, and since I'd had the experience of worsening cancer being overlooked, I decided to be proactive and see my orthopedic oncologist. An X-ray revealed that there was disease progression in the head of my right femur, the large upper bone of the leg. The doctors agreed that there was a possible fracture in the femur head and they were concerned that the instability of the bone could cause me to lose the ability to walk in the future. They recommended that I go through a "nail procedure." A titanium rod would be driven into the entire femur leg bone with pins embedded in two places to secure it.

More titanium? I thought as they explained the procedure.

Only six weeks after the spinal fusion, I had this next surgery. It was a much shorter procedure, only scheduled for 30 minutes. And to my delight, I knew the anesthesiologist from having worked with him at my previous job. He had been my absolute favorite person to work with and it was another reminder that God was with me every single step of the way.

Chuck

Five years earlier, I had spent a lot of time in the pool after my spinal collapse. I loved how it took the weight off my body and allowed me to stretch and move. Hannah is also a big fan of the water, but she was told not to get the 60-staple incision wet. I was in our home office when Hannah hollered from the other room that she had ordered pizza and the app said the driver was just a block away. Mid-day pizza? It sounded good to me. The next thing I knew an Amazon delivery driver was outside. I told Hannah we got a delivery, but it didn't look like pizza.

"Can you please open it?" she asked.

I took my pocket knife out and ran it along the tape. Inside the box was a pool float that looked like a giant slice of pizza. We both started laughing. She told me that since she couldn't get her incision wet, she decided to get a pool float to keep her out of the water. I helped Hannah out of her wheelchair down the few steps into the pool. It was tricky getting her on the pizza float on the first try, but once she was on it she seemed free. She said it was the only place that her back did not hurt. After two days, I noticed she was using her hands while floating to move around the pool. This was amazing and I found myself standing there with my camera and big tears rolling down my face. Thinking about everything she had been through, her drive to get a tiny bit better everyday was inspiring.

Although our borrowed wheelchair was pretty old, felt like it weighed about two hundred pounds, *and* was too wide for some of our doorways, it allowed us to get her out of bed and sometimes out of the house. I liked the thought of her having some independence, so I took the next step and began researching electric wheelchairs. I found a used one that needed new batteries and a bath. We loved that it was small and could go just about anywhere. I bought metal ramps so she could get out of the house completely on her own. Another laugh/cry moment was when she went on her own, a few houses away, to our cousin Heather's to borrow some ketchup. It was like taking your child to the bus stop on the first day and that feeling of letting go as the bus drove off. She waved really big as she drove down the alley to the street, took a right turn, and then went out of sight.

I loved the independence the electric wheelchair gave her. I lowered everything in the kitchen so she could reach the tea, cereal, and snacks she liked. She even put half of the dishes away from the dishwasher because they went on shelves she could reach. I loved watching her go.

Her view of the temporary nature of that wheelchair while going through this really difficult time is a crucial example for everyone reading this book. Hannah's concept of *I am here in this hard space but not for long* is so beautiful and awe-inspiring to me.

We began having discussions about future speaking events and travel when she was up to it. I loved setting goals together. Then we received an email that surprised both of us. It was from Harley-Davidson of Scottsdale. They were searching for a cancer foundation to join them for an event on June 6th—National Cancer Survivors Day. I called them to explain that since I was a Stage 4 survivor, it was one of my favorite days of the year. They asked if we would serve as the honorary cancer foundation for their event. After getting on the same page, our answer was yes. We only had four weeks to pump this up. Since Hannah was supposed to rest in her post-surgery recovery mode, I called on Debbie from our Living Hope Cancer Foundation advisory board for some help. Deb has great energy, so the two of us went into action and by June 6th, we had over 30 businesses involved, and the event programs and t-shirts were donated. Man, did National Cancer Survivors Day with Harley-Davidson of Scottsdale fall into place! They fired up two huge grills and supplied the food and hired a DJ for the event. People approached us and explained they were cancer survivors, which led to conversations, hugs and us giving them a free event t-shirt. Hannah and I spoke about our lives dealing with cancer, our faith, and how God was keeping us strong. We literally spent the day hugging people. That is part of our job. Passing out love and hugs.

Hannah

I finally got the okay to start chemotherapy again. This time I was at an entirely new oncology practice with an entirely new treatment plan. At the advice of my spinal surgeon who was appalled at my previous lack of care, he pointed me to a new oncologist. After interviewing him, Chuck and I agreed this was a better plan for me. Even as a nurse and playing constant advocate for myself, I was finding holes in my care and God was guiding us to new paths. I began new chemotherapy towards the end of May.

Meanwhile, as I was recuperating from the latest surgery, I could feel how much trauma this had all been to my body.

I was losing a lot of weight as a result of nausea caused by the large number of chemicals circulating through my body post surgery. I struggled with appetite and eating became a chore. Trust me when I say that I had never had that problem before. I weighed myself one day and the scale showed that I was down 25 pounds. I hadn't seen 129 pounds since I was in the 8th grade. At six feet tall, that was seriously underweight, unless I was looking to be a supermodel. My mom became concerned after talking over the phone and called a family meeting with Chuck and me. She and my dad offered to come and visit for ten days to help cook and clean. At this point, Chuck needed a serious caregiver break and I needed my mom's home cooking.

By the time she left, I had gained four pounds and was well on my way to healing. We had spent every morning walking and talking in the pool doing my physical therapy exercises, and I was eating approximately every two hours just like a teenage boy. I was ravenous. I'm pretty sure I ate organic homemade mashed potatoes every single day for ten days straight. And I wasn't mad about it!

Just three days later, my best friend Linda was scheduled to fly in from Pennsylvania to visit and take care of me. I love how God set this up as part of the plan for me to heal and regain my strength post-surgery. The second tenet that we teach when we cancer coach is to surround yourself with the love of family and friends. God created us for community and this was exactly what we both needed to heal and be refreshed.

CHAPTER TWENTY-TWO

From Wheelchair To Ebike

Hannah

The easiest thing for me to do at home was to hop on my motorized wheelchair and wheel around the house. I was still experiencing some deep muscle pain near the surgical site and my natural tendency was pain avoidance. But I knew that I needed to start challenging myself. Our foundation was growing and we were continuing to coach cancer patients. And since you can do that from any location, when our friends offered us their Flagstaff vacation home, we jumped at the chance to escape the Phoenix heat for a much-needed writing retreat. I knew that my wheelchair would be difficult to use in their house, so I made a plan to only use my walker. Chuck arranged for us to temporarily join an Athletic Club nearby the house with pool access so that I could continue to walk in the pool and do my exercises while he swam his daily mile.

I came home from that trip able to walk short distances while continuing to use my wheelchair for trips to the grocery store and to chemotherapy. Those longer distances still felt impossible to travel on my own two feet. But I was moving in the right direction.

Our friend Barbara had invited us to join her family at a beach house in California several months prior. I was determined to go for Chuck's sake. The beach was his place to find "rest." He craved ocean air and I wanted so much for him to feel that. I pushed myself harder than I would have for myself and said yes to the journey. When we got to the house, we saw that it had two large levels with nineteen stairs in between. I knew it would be physically challenging for me to move between the two levels, but I also knew that I was going to figure out a way to meet that challenge. I hadn't climbed stairs for a year since our trip to Ohio. After all, we didn't have stairs in our home, and everywhere else had an elevator. My motorized wheelchair had made my life easier the past few months. But when faced with reality, I amazingly climbed those stairs one step at a time! Tears sprang to my eyes when I reached the top. I had done it and would continue to go up and down those stairs several times a day. I was using muscles I hadn't used in months. I was getting stronger, testing my limits, and surpassing what I thought I could do.

Chuck

I watched Hannah go from a wheelchair to walking and then to slowly climbing the stairs. Being her partner, her coach, and her number one fan meant I was there to support her all the way. But I also was prepared to help if she tried something and needed to take a step back. Even though I had loaded her electric wheelchair for the car trip to Ventura, she never touched it. Not only did she take her time and carefully walk around the huge beachfront house, she told me on the second day there that she wanted to walk on the beach even if she wouldn't be able to go far. Sand is unstable and I did not let her get too far from me, but we both had tears in our eyes as she walked out to the ocean waves, stopped and raised her hands, and thanked God for our lives. The third morning in Ventura, she told me that she wanted to see what it felt like to ride her ebike. Even though these amazing bikes have an electric motor that provides assistance, I worried that she wouldn't be able to stabilize herself and the bike when she would come upon a traffic light or group of people. Remember, it had been less than three months since she had a spinal surgery and a titanium rod placed into her right femur, so we could not risk an injury or setback. I did a quick walk around checking the tires, making sure the folding lock mechanisms were in place and charged up. We kept the seat low so she could put her feet down if needed. We started out by crossing the street onto the beach lane going south on a service road that ran next to the Ventura oceanfront. I looked over to see how she was doing and my tough girl was crying. I shed my own big tears at the thought of what she had been through and of having to watch my wife deal with cancer, pain, treatment, and surgeries. Yet here she was on a bike, cruising along the coast. She looked over at me and reminded me it had been six months since she was on her bike.

In my mind, I thought about how she had just gone from a wheelchair to an ebike. That says so much about her spirit, her faith, her drive, and her ability to set goals and achieve them. We also had thousands of people all over the world, thanks to social media, who were watching, commenting, and praying for Hannah. I watched her confidence increase mile by mile.

You don't know your limits if you never try.

The next day we got on the bikes again, rode six miles north into the beach city of Ventura, and ended up at a great fish restaurant on the pier. We had a great lunch date and rode back towards the house watching the surfers rip it up along the coast for a total round trip of twelve miles. The rest of the day we relaxed sitting at the ocean with our laptops and thinking how our story would make a great book or movie. Then we laughed and said, "Nobody would believe it!"

Hannah

At the end of our visit, we stopped in Carlsbad, a beach town near where we had honeymooned. We had fond memories of riding our beach cruisers down the Pacific Coast Highway and, in a small way, it felt like I had come full circle. Here I was one and a half years later, having gone through some of the toughest physical challenges of my life, back on a bike. I couldn't have imagined it a few months earlier during those dark days of recovery when the pain and nausea wouldn't subside. It was hard to see past my present situation when a big day meant getting to the recliner in the living room. I remember my mom telling me that I needed to let "time" heal my physical wounds. It wasn't until six weeks after surgery that I would notice any real improvements. And it was almost eight weeks after my last surgery that I first got back on my bike. Although I had enjoyed the flat stretches of biking in Ventura, the hilly oceanfront roads of Carlsbad and several towns south were more challenging, and I felt like I hit a wall. Even though I was on an electric bike with pedal assist, I hadn't factored in the steep climbs up and down the hills. We spent an hour sitting at the beach and then stopped at a cute cafe for lunch. By early afternoon, I knew I was too tired to bike our way back home. Our failsafe had been to take the Coaster train home to our friend's house and I was happy to use that lifeline. Even though I couldn't do all of the activities that I normally could do, and it felt disappointing, I recognized that I had to find my limits. If I didn't test my limits, I wouldn't know what I was actually capable of nor would I see my incredible progress. That had been a significant factor in my recovery for the past year. I had to keep trying. Every day I held onto one of my favorite verses: Philippians 4:13 "I can do all things through Christ who gives me strength." *All things* didn't just mean having a good attitude or getting out of bed each day. It also meant going on a bike ride or getting in the pool to exercise my body. God promised to help me in those areas, too. I love that I get to live in the supernatural and live out my life in His strength. It's been the greatest part of my healing—trusting Him to physically strengthen me for everyday tasks.

Chuck

Being the guy that goes nonstop most days, I had to watch for signs with Hannah so I knew when to regroup and slow down. There were times I would suggest things to her and get shut down fast. "I'm not going to be hiking anytime soon," she would say. I know it was tough on her, but I also knew I had to drive the bus, plant little things in her mind, and keep her thinking. With Hannah and me being so close, I felt everything she was going through. The physical pain my wife was dealing with tested my faith. But the mental struggle people go through when facing a cancer diagnosis or other challenge can be the biggest and hardest part. I have told many people that watching Hannah's pain and struggle was more difficult than suffering my own broken back, going through Stage 4 cancer, and having to fight my way back.

That day when we went out on our bikes along the ocean was so exciting as we took in the views and celebrated the fact that Hannah was back on her ebike. The first few hours were everything we imagined. But soon the hills, the traffic, and tons of people moving around a beach town on a summer Saturday became too much for me, much less Hannah who was just starting to venture back into the world.

As she started to "hit the wall," I felt every bit of it. A few tears fell and she said, "I want my body back."

The only thing I can do at times like those is to hug her until she is ready to push a little further. I constantly let her know that I have her back. I love doing life with Hannah, whether we're sitting in a chemo room or sitting at the beach. The only thing I can do when the emotions kick in is to live in that moment. I used to run from emotional things and did not want anyone to think I wasn't tough. But being that way got me nowhere. We soon learned to keep a box of tissues handy and apologize when we hug and get tears and snot on each other. It's all good.

CHAPTER TWENTY-THREE

The Body & The Mind

Chuck

I watched Hannah go from being in so much pain that she could not sit up in bed, to pointing at her wheelchair and telling me it was time to get rid of it. I watched her power through pain and challenges and go from a wheelchair to twelve miles along the beach on her ebike. I watched her go from crying out in pain in the middle of the night, "God how much more can I take?" to just three months later, kayaking with me on the lake. How amazing and powerful is the human mind if we have control of it?

Based on our personal journeys with Stage 4 cancer and meeting thousands of people who are dealing with cancer of all types, surgeries of all kinds, and other physical challenges, I am blown away by how amazing the human body is. I've seen people go through car accidents, severe burns, illnesses that took limbs, and the effects of cancer. Usually, the human body responds by losing weight, shutting down, making people sleep for days, or go into a high fever. Why do all of these things happen? God has engineered amazing human bodies for us. I also believe that God gave us the intelligence to study books and become doctors and create a chemotherapy product to kill some types of cancer. But we are still in a big race to figure out the cell mutation that robs the body and pushes it into decline until it can no longer support life.

As the research continues, we are amazed at how the human body starts to respond and recover. We call these daily miracles. Some miracles are fast and appear to be bigger, but a fast miracle or a slow miracle is still a miracle. My miracle in 2015 was a fast miracle as I went from cancer spreading throughout my body to a clean scan three months later. Did I still have to do my part by juicing, using essential oils, and doing physical workouts to speed up my recovery? Absolutely. This is the reason we coach everyone to *get up and live* because the body needs fuel and movement to respond, recover, and find its new normal.

Hannah's miracle has been a slow miracle. She has been through ridiculous damage from cancer, as well as the side effects of treatment chemicals and procedures. Doctors have told us that Stage 4 cancer is terminal. I'm not sure I understand their definition of the word *terminal*. I was told I was terminal in 2015. I do know that *all* of us are terminal. There are no guarantees for any of us and that is why we give all of this to God, live in the moment, and live our best lives for Him every day. There are things the body will do to fight back and recover. We have found that nutrition and exercise are both factors. What is something else that is a huge factor? The power of the human mind. Something in the mind can remind us that a bad situation is just temporary and that we can make it through this. I wish I knew why some people have this and others do not. I remember being down forty pounds and being told I had only three months to live, yet jumping in the car every day to go to the gym. Even when I was told I was dying and I was so weak from cancer and chemo, I would walk into the gym, stick the pin in under the top plate, say a quick prayer to God to hold me together, and then make sure I did my workout. I fought against people who told me not to overdo it. I fought my own mental challenges and told myself that it was mind over matter and to get after it!

Hannah

I can't remember ever not having the will to fight. I've been through meningitis, a Stage 3 breast cancer diagnosis, multiple surgeries (I've honestly lost count), and a metastatic breast cancer diagnosis. It's never occurred to me not to give it my all and continue fighting. I think a lot of that has to do with my faith. I believe that God's will for us is to have a healthy and abundant life. It's the enemy that comes in seeking to kill and destroy us, especially when we are doing good for God's kingdom. John 10:10 NLT "The thief's purpose is to steal and kill and destroy. My purpose is to give them a rich and satisfying life."

I've mentioned before that this is so much more than our physical circumstances; it's a spiritual warfare. We are spirit beings living with earthly bodies, and God calls us to be spirit-minded. It's entirely changed how I approach my earthly body when I recognize that it follows what my spirit is doing. If my spirit is at peace, my body is too. I'm not stressed or anxious in my body when I'm not stressed or anxious in my spirit. That reality is helping me focus more on my spiritual life, feeding that part of me with the truth about what God says, and growing my relationship with Him.

I need to keep taking care of my physical body. Some days that looks like resting in my recliner, but as I am getting stronger, I'm adding in the physical tasks that I am able to accomplish. It began with walking in the pool, stretching, doing small exercises in bed, and gradually adding more walking and actual movement.

Nourishing my body with nutrient-dense foods has helped my energy level and healing. Even though my swallowing problems keep me from eating a lot of crunchy raw foods, I have found that juicing is an easy way to get raw fuel directly into my cells. I love to cook simple ingredient meals that taste good. Chuck doesn't mind it either!

A big part of my healing has come from being surrounded by a community that loves me: my husband Chuck, my neighbors, my pastors, my friends from church, and quite a few local people that only know my name yet still send us gift cards or meals. God created us for community and we should respond in a way that we can serve each other and be served when we need it. We aren't supposed to do this life alone. I can't wait for the day that I can physically give back in that way. But meanwhile, God has gifted me the ability to serve people from my bed or couch by encouraging them through their cancer journeys. We love when it can be done in person, but talking, texting, and messaging is the next best thing and it's convenient. We all need that kind word and reminder that we aren't alone in the hard spaces of life. I get to do that every day. We both do.

Chuck

So let's not underestimate prayer, love, the power of the mind, and how amazing the human body is. It is very important that when you have a healthcare situation, you have both a medical plan and a personal plan. Do not underestimate what happens in the human body when the fight is turned on. And if God's plan for you is a short plan, would you rather spend your last years/months/days in bed, or outside breathing fresh air, watching the sunset, and walking on the beach? Live each moment and never pass up an opportunity to say *I love you*.

CHAPTER TWENTY-FOUR

Giving God the Glory in Our Story

Hannah

Life with my best friend has been undeniably adventurous. We each add our own twist to the relationship, although I think my contribution *could* be less fracture-filled going forward. I don't think Chuck was looking for all those kinds of surprises when he said "I do" on our wedding day. But he's taken them in stride because of the very fact that he has learned from the lessons God was teaching us through the trials. He stayed in a posture of *Help me, Lord* as he watched me in pain and had to deny himself to serve me. He isn't the same man that I married. He's grown so much in all the ways that matter.

We both recognize that every step of our lives is ordained by God. It's been such a relief to rest in that reality and to know that He has a much better way of writing our story than we do, one that brings Him glory. You might pause and question how in the world I could say that statement with all the pain and drama of the past five years. But without them, I truly would not have learned about surrender and peace. I wouldn't have learned the importance of living a Spirit-led life. I wouldn't have given Chuck the time of day out of fear of another relationship that could fail. I wouldn't be walking in my calling of serving other cancer patients and their families as I coached them on how to thrive with cancer. I likely wouldn't have survived the cancer progression last year. Mindset is everything. If I wasn't Spirit-minded, I would just be wandering aimlessly, stressed out, and *freaking* out. I was in that place four years ago and have slowly been learning how to trust God every step of the way. I've been learning to give Him my day and ask Him to lead me to whoever and whatever I need to do that day. It has changed my life. I say "yes" every day. Whether it's facing a surgery, another chemo treatment, or a thrilling gondola ride in the Arizona mountains. It's all about the people I get to interact with and point to Jesus. He's my only hope in this life.

I have no idea what tomorrow holds. I could get hit by a bus or live another 45 years cancer-free. But, you see, it doesn't really matter to me because God holds my future in His hands and I know I am totally safe and secure in His grasp. I don't have to worry about anything. He's faithful and *with* me. He has given me a loving husband that loves Him, too. I'm looking forward to being healed completely. One of the verses He has given me over and over is Psalm 118:17 "I will not die; instead I will live to tell what the Lord has done." That verse has been proclaimed to me multiple times by strangers who don't know me. It's this beautiful promise-filled reminder of my job here on earth; whether I'm fulfilling it on stage, through my books, in a social media post, or standing in the middle of a clothing store aisle sharing our miracle stories with strangers. However that looks today.

And I'll be cancer-free for eternity and I can't wait.

Chuck

At 55 years old watching time fly by, I had been praying for a partner that I could make laugh with my silly sense of humor and make memories with. But I was starting to think that dream would never happen until God blessed me with Hannah, the perfect match for me in every way. We are gradually changing and growing into this spectacular couple, beyond my imagination. When we sit or drive and talk for hours, we never get tired of each other, and in those conversations we can obviously see that we are melding into one. One of the most important and beautiful things about what makes us work is that we have our own individual relationships with God. Jesus is our first love because worldly things are temporary. If you have idols or rely on a person to take care of you, someday you will get a wake-up call. So if you read this entire book, walk away with this one important piece of wisdom: *run towards God*. Look over your shoulder every once in a while to see who is keeping up, then run faster. Look over and see the one who is keeping up, doing the same thing as you are, and marry them. Does this mean there will not be struggles and hurdles? No, but it means that when the world gets heavy you will have someone there that knows you, understands you, and wants the best for you.

None of this could have ever happened without God's plan being way bigger than we could comprehend. It took a journey with end-of-life Stage 4 cancer to get my attention. Give it all to God. He gave His son Jesus to walk this earth and be the greatest teacher of all time. He gave His life because He loved us and wanted to forgive our sins. Unconditional love is what I am trying to show Hannah, the cancer patients we coach, and every single person God is putting in our path.

We hope our story about two people diagnosed with Stage 4 cancer who dramatically changed their lives has the power to also touch your life. I have no idea what tomorrow will bring, but one of the biggest lessons that you learn when your mind is opened by hearing the words *you have cancer* is to let go of all of the wasted time and focus on what you are truly passionate about. That may be as simple as a hug and an *I love you* or a sunset at your favorite spot. Roses smell different. A sunset looks different. A hug feels different. God allowed us to go through a journey with cancer to share this journey with you, so that you can acquire wisdom and put it to use wherever you are. We have been down in the mud on our knees so many times in our lives that we have no problem getting down on our knees in *your* mud to give you a hug, to tell you our story, and tell you how a relationship with Jesus changed our lives and *saved* our lives.

God gave me the gift of being a warrior. It starts with helping my wife and giving it my all. Now I can come looking for you, whoever you are. God gave me this ridiculous energy and a big heart full of love. I don't let the little things distract me because I know the plan now. God told me to tell my story to as many people as I possibly can and bring them to Him. Now Hannah is part of my story and this is why the Living Hope Cancer Foundation was born. How many people can we love and help in the scariest time of their lives? The question that we most often hear is: What do I do with cancer? I have kids, grandkids, and a beautiful spouse, but I didn't plan for this!

We understand because we have been there and asked those same questions. Hannah and I took all of our personal experiences and launched a nonprofit to help as many people as we possibly can by coaching cancer patients and their families to keep a positive mindset through this tough time. We work hard with clients and we work hard building a cancer foundation so it will be around long after we are gone. We get to do all of this while Hannah is on a journey with Stage 4 triple negative breast cancer, sometimes while in agonizing pain, going through surgeries, treatments, and their side effects. We were told that her healing would come from the faith of thousands of people all over the world praying for her and now we get to experience that.

Hannah

Chuck and I have huge God-given dreams. We are dream chasers partnering with God to accomplish what He has put inside of our hearts. And we live in His economy, letting Him provide our every need on a daily basis while we are on a mission for Him. Sometimes that can feel scary to me when the old parts of me want to control my situation. But then we receive an unexpected check in the mail and it's a gentle reminder from my Provider to just trust Him.

Just trust Him for every single thing.

We have dreams to tour around the country in an RV to share our cancer ministry, inspire churches and groups with public speaking, and share our books and stories. We have a goal to open a cancer retreat in Arizona and eventually replicate that model in other states. We want to create a coaching curriculum to train and certify other cancer survivors who want to help coach. We will continue to build our video resource library with relevant topical video series, like our Cancer Roadmap Project, so that we can help as many cancer patients as possible navigate this crazy journey with cancer. We also have plans to create a written curriculum for cancer patients to help them on their journey. We will keep designing new apparel to sell in our online store. And there is always more fundraising, more grant writing, more patients to coach off the couch to *get up and live,* and more caregivers to encourage.

It's the unique space that God has called us to fill and we want to keep saying **yes** to Him every day.

Every day, we **get up and live** together, hand in hand, for His glory.

LIVING HOPE
CANCER FOUNDATION

VISIT WWW.GETUPANDLIVE.ORG **TO JOIN THE**

CANCER ROADMAP PROJECT

AND MORE!

- Resources
- Free Video Coaching
- Donate

- Find Community
- Get Swag
- Contact Chuck and Hannah